MAGICAL PATHS

MAGICAL PATHS

LABYRINTHS AND MAZES IN THE 21ST CENTURY

Jeff Saward

MITCHELL BEAZLEY

To Kimberly, without
whose help none of
this would have been
possible

MAGICAL PATHS
First published in 2002
by Mitchell Beazley, an imprint
of Octopus Publishing Group Ltd,
2–4 Heron Quays, London E14 4JP

First published in paperback in 2008

ISBN 978 1 84533 422 2

A CIP catalogue copy of this book
is available from the British Library

Senior Editor   **Michèle Byam**
Executive Art Editor   **Christie Cooper**
Design   **Lovelock and Co.**
Contributing Editor   **Selina Mumford**
Production Controller   **Alix McCulloch**
Picture Researcher   **Juliet Duff**
Indexer   **Laura Hicks**

Set in Frutiger

Printed and bound in China by
Toppan Printing Company Limited

Distributed in the United States and
Canada by Sterling Publishing Co. Inc.,
387 Park Avenue South, New York
NY 10016-8810

HALF TITLE PAGE *The 1997 "Labyrinthus"
maize maze, Reignac-sur-Indre, France.*
OPPOSITE TITLE PAGE *The Darwin
Garden Labyrinth, Ilkley, England,
constructed May 2000.*
RIGHT *Stone labyrinth on the island of Blå
Jungfrun, Sweden.*

CONTENTS

INTRODUCTION

BELOW *Situated on a remote island in the White Sea in Arctic Russia, this labyrinth formed of boulders could be two thousand years old. This classical design, with its single pathway, has been used for thousands of years.*

THE INWARD PATH

Surely, if you are reading this book it is because you, too, are fascinated by mazes and labyrinths. Whether you consider yourself an old-hand at solving the winding ways of your favourite hedge maze, or have ever tried to navigate your way through one of the fiendish maize mazes that have sprung up since the early 1990s in farmers' fields, you may wonder how these remarkable structures have developed, who builds them and why? Perhaps you have encountered a labyrinth in your local church or cathedral, or have stumbled across one of the many surviving ancient turf or stone labyrinths that are found in often remote locations around the countryside or on some wild shoreline. If so, you are not alone in your fascination.

Within the past twenty-five years or so, the popularity of mazes and labyrinths in a diverse range of settings around the world has increased to an extraordinary degree. This dramatic revival started slowly at first, with a few people experimenting with new design concepts and materials. This had happened before when, at different places and points in time, maze crazes had flourished and faded, only to spring back to life in a different culture with a slightly different take on the original concept. However, since 1992 a remarkable renaissance of mazes and labyrinths has blossomed in a fashion that no one could have imagined.

Barely a summer now goes by without our hearing about another record-breaking maize maze that is featured in the media, another stately home or entertainment park that has installed a splendid new hedge maze, or a television gardening program that creates a small floral labyrinth to enhance a suburban garden or back yard. This current love affair with all things amazing and labyrinthine extends across the board; consider, for instance, the number of computer games that revolve around solving a maze, however huge and bewildering, to find the hidden treasure, save the princess, or dispatch the villains that lurk within. Watch for them as metaphors for confusing matters in legal and financial advertizing. Mazes and labyrinths became an intriguing phenomenon of the late 20th century, and now, in the early 21st century, they continue to capture the imagination in ever more surprising ways.

As one of the people involved since the late 1970s in this revival of mazes and labyrinths, primarily as an observer and commentator, I have watched these developments unfold from the edge of the field, while editing the subject's house journal, and researching the long and complex history of mazes and labyrinths. Over the years, my travels have taken me around the world to visit and document mazes and labyrinths, old and new, and I have had the opportunity to meet and speak with many of the key players in the field. Within the pages of this book, I hope to be able to shed some light on the reasons and directions that this remarkable and amazing revival has taken.

MAZES OR LABYRINTHS?

Mazes and labyrinths – why are there two terms in popular use and just what is the difference between them? This is often the first question that journalists and curious newcomers to the field ask. Current literature and news reports frequently confound and confuse the two, but designers and owners alike are often passionate about which is which. Look up the words in a dictionary and you will probably conclude that a maze is a labyrinth, and a labyrinth is a maze. Maybe you will find some mention of hedges, Minotaurs, or Hampton Court. Before continuing, we need to define what constitutes a maze or a labyrinth, and why these two terms are used, often interchangeably, and what makes up the real difference between them.

Throughout much of the non-English speaking world, practically every maze mentioned in this book would be called a "labyrinth," for the word "maze" is a peculiarly English word of medieval origin that refers to a state of confusion, from which the term "amazed" is derived. To be confused, let alone amazed, there must be some element of choice in the pathway that you are following, some opportunity to become bewildered. Many current writers, designers, and commentators within the field have taken this as a point of definition:

To qualify as a maze, a design must have choices in the pathway.

This category includes most of the modern installations in tourist attractions and entertainments parks, which exist solely for the purpose of perplexing potential visitors.

But what are we to make of the earliest examples of the type known as hedge mazes? Many of these were planted to designs, then current, on the floors of cathedrals; they have but one path that leads inexorably from the entrance to the goal, albeit by the most complex and winding of routes. These designs were known at the time as "labyrinths" and were developments of simpler labyrinth designs that had been in existence for thousands of years. All have just the single path, however confusing it might seem. This has also been taken as a definition of this style:

To qualify as a labyrinth, a design should have but one path.

Of course, as in life, nothing is quite this simple. The dividing line between what constitutes a maze or a labyrinth can sometimes become blurred and difficult to define. By and large, the differences are clear for all to see, even though occasionally a labyrinth can have more than one pathway and a maze can lead nowhere but to its goal. The intent of the design is usually clear enough to allow the simple categorization of any example you may encounter, and, on the whole, I have adhered to these definitions throughout this book.

THE LONG PATH

The history of mazes and labyrinths has undergone periods of fast growth and development, when they have found new acceptance and meaning in a rapidly developing social context. Each episode has created a wealth of new labyrinths to be encountered, experienced, and studied. From the Bronze Age settlements on the Atlantic coastline and the shores of the Mediterranean Sea, through the Roman Empire and the medieval Christian Church to modern usage in both secular and spiritual contexts, labyrinths are everywhere. The archetypal labyrinth symbol occurs from Iceland, Scandinavia and Arctic Russia, throughout Europe, north Africa and the Middle East down into the Indian subcontinent and Indonesia. It is also found in a historical context in the American Southwest, Mexico, and Brazil.

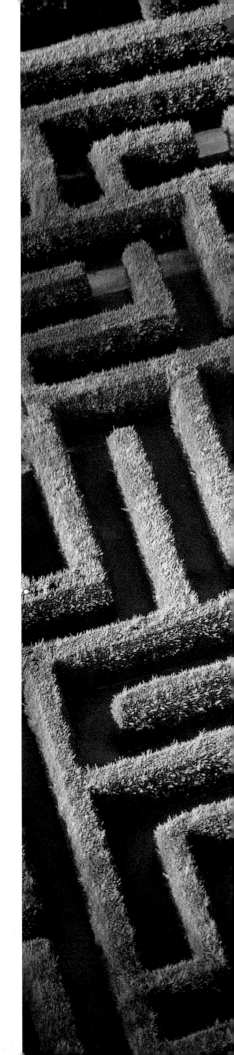

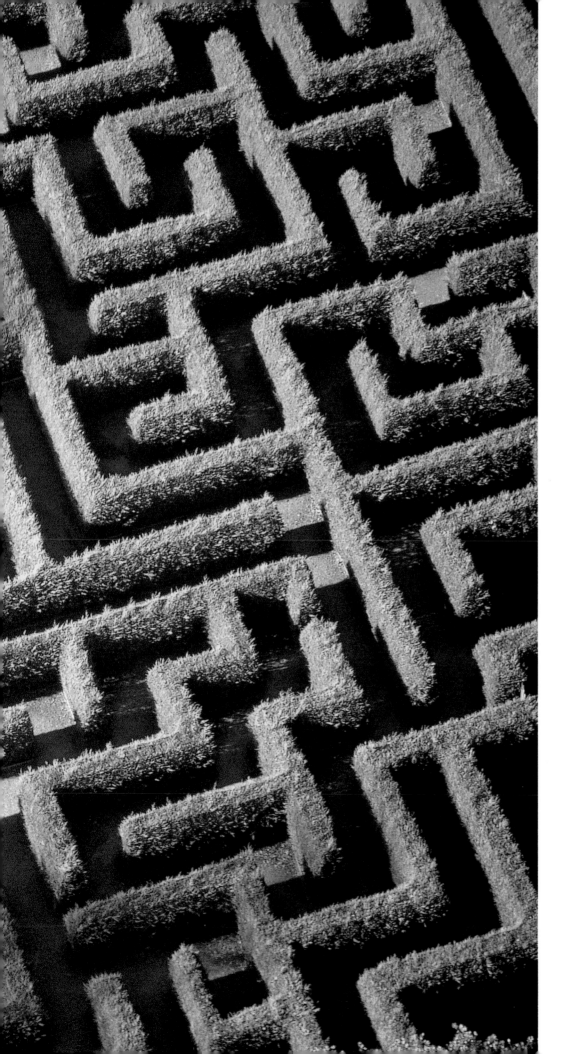

LEFT *The branching pathways of the latest generation of puzzle mazes include some with extremely complex designs. While many modern materials are now used for their construction, the traditional hedge mazes remain a popular form.*

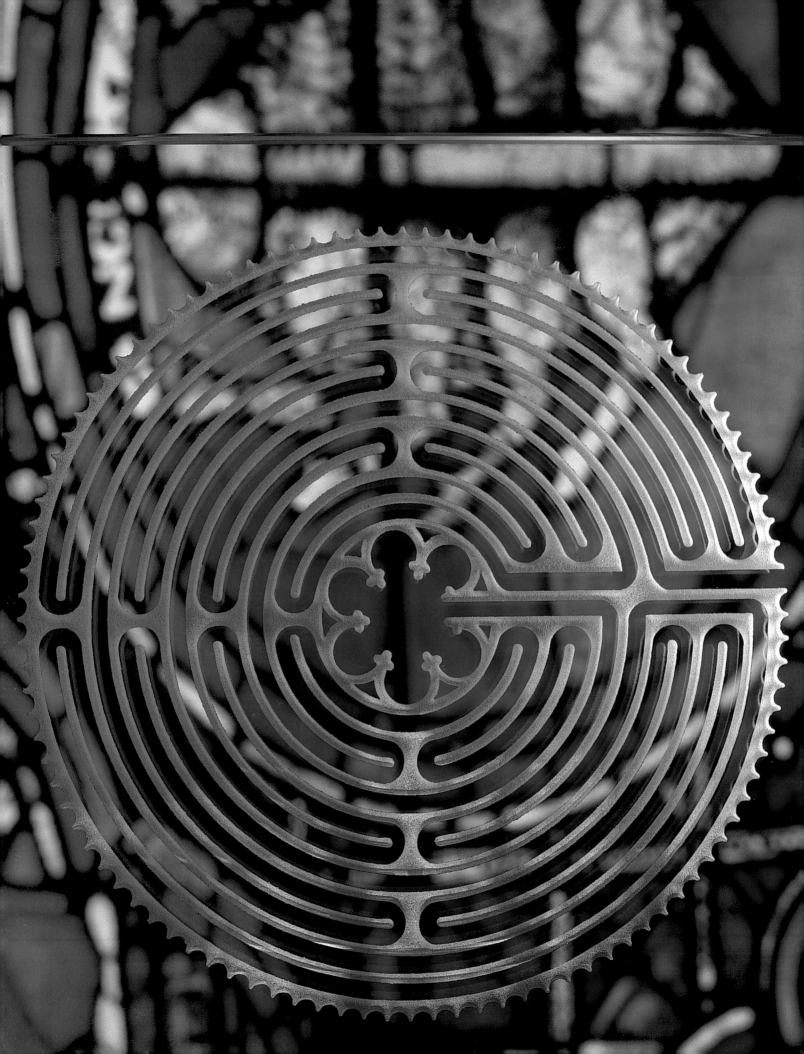

Throughout this vast range, the labyrinth takes many forms and is constructed in various materials. How and when this symbol came to be found in such diverse locations remains a puzzle for labyrinth scholars. From the earliest examples to modern times, the designs of these labyrinths have undergone a number of evolutionary changes, gradually developing into ever more complex forms, although the original archetypal labyrinth symbol continually re-surfaces, partly due to its ease of construction, and because it is the starting point for all other labyrinth designs. During the late medieval and renaissance periods, the labyrinth became a popular feature of garden design and rapidly evolved into the first true puzzle mazes, usually constructed of hedges. It is only during the last century or so that complex puzzle mazes, utilizing various construction materials, have appeared on the scene, with the majority of new developments and innovations taking place within the last twenty-five years. Here at the beginning of the 21st century, we are in the midst of one of the largest and most widespread of these developmental events so far.

THE CURRENT REVIVAL

At the start of the 1980s there were maybe fifty public mazes and labyrinths in the British Isles. Now, at the start of the 21st century, that number stands at one hundred and fifty and counting. A decade ago there were only a handful of labyrinths in churches in America, now there are hundreds. The maize mazes that are a regular feature of summer cornfields across Europe and America were unknown prior to 1993. The exponential increase in numbers, complexity, and materials employed to create this new generation of mazes and labyrinths is truly remarkable, and extremely difficult at first sight to document.

Many thousands of new mazes and labyrinths have been built since the 1980s. The purpose of this book is not to provide any form of comprehensive guide to their location, as they are simply too numerous, and continue to appear apace. Instead, I hope to identify the main themes and players that run through this seemingly inextricably tangled maze of materials, designs, and designers. With an initial historical background against which to place many of these modern maze creations in context, the story of this most recent explosion of interest in mazes and labyrinths is much like the designs of those very same mazes – full of twists and turns, and pathways that invariably come full circle.

The public enjoyment of and rising enthusiasm for mazes and labyrinths has developed in interesting ways in recent years. Two particular strands deserve special mention: the enthralment with puzzle mazes and the rediscovery of the labyrinth.

The fascination with multicursal mazes, exemplified by the increasingly innovative puzzle mazes constructed in cornfields, leisure parks, and gardens, has sparked a plethora of new design concepts and construction materials employed to provide amusement and amazement. Both children and adults enjoy the challenge of getting lost as well as the satisfaction of reaching a goal, and the addition of interactivity and imaginative design features have turned mazes into a venue for family entertainment, offering exciting opportunities for exploring and experiencing the unknown in settings where age has little advantage, and child-like play is actively encouraged.

Alongside this very public resurgence of mazes we have witnessed a rather more discreet revival of unicursal labyrinths in private locations. These labyrinths are also appearing with increasing frequency in churches, gardens, and as landscape art installations for more public use. Many hundreds of labyrinths have been constructed in the last decade throughout the Americas and Europe, and they are now appearing as far afield as New Zealand. Here in Britain, they are becoming a feature for the small garden, public and private – recently popularized by television gardening programs and magazine articles. This current revival is, however, just the latest episode in a long sequence of cyclical flowerings of the labyrinth that can be traced back in time to the 2nd millennium BC, a history that now spans five separate millennia.

REFLECTING ON THE PATH

Yet not all of this activity is concerned with the construction of new mazes and labyrinths. A fresh realization of the importance of historic examples has developed in recent years. Many overgrown hedge mazes are being restored and replanted, and ancient turf labyrinths and stone labyrinths are now receiving the care they need. These important developments ensure the survival of these labyrinths for future generations. Much of this success is due to the tireless efforts of researchers, academics, and enthusiasts, who have been pooling their information over the past two decades to allow a new understanding of the diversity, distribution, and history of mazes and labyrinths to develop. In the last last ten years several important studies have been published and this flurry of labyrinthine literature has brought the subject to the attention of an ever-wider readership and inspired a new generation of enthusiasts to continue and expand the work.

Throughout the long history of mazes and labyrinths, whenever and wherever society is undergoing rapid change and development, the labyrinth, in one form or another, has blossomed. The expansion of worldwide tourism and growing leisure time has created an environment with many opportunities for mazes that are increasingly complex, whether symbolically, intellectually, or technologically, in order to entice and ensnare a new generation of visitors. Contrastingly, in these uncertain and confusing times, humanity is once again seeking the sure path of the labyrinth, reflecting as it does the journey of life in which one step is taken at a time, as the turns and setbacks of life in the modern world are negotiated.

Jeff Saward, Thundersley, England, May 2002

RIGHT *The fashion for wooden panel mazes that swept Japan during the 1980s resulted in over 200 examples being built within a few years. This craze soon waned, however, and only a few of these mazes survive.*

A BRIEF HISTORY

The story of mazes and labyrinths is as long and tortuous as their plans might suggest. For nearly four thousand years people have been using labyrinths for a multitude of purposes, constructing them in almost as many forms. From a simple symbol scratched on stone to the labyrinths that fill the floors of the great Gothic cathedrals, the labyrinth has always found its symbolic niche in society. From these basic labyrinths have evolved complex puzzle mazes that are familiar worldwide.

THE FIRST LABYRINTHS

The first chapter of this long and complex story takes us back to the dusty shores of the Mediterranean Sea and the hills along the Atlantic coastlines of prehistoric Europe. Sometime near the end of the Neolithic period or at the start of the Bronze Age, during the early 2nd millennium BC, hunters and traders travelling in the region started to engrave the earliest of the labyrinth symbols on rockfaces adjacent to their favoured hunting grounds and beside tracks leading through mountain passes. This specific design – known as the "classical" labyrinth symbol – is found during prehistory from one end of the Mediterranean to the other. Many examples, such as those carved on rockfaces, are extremely difficult to date; labyrinths found among rock-art inscriptions in Galicia, northwestern Spain, are currently considered to be some of the earliest examples, tentatively dated to perhaps as early as c.2000 BC. However, other examples, found scratched as graffiti on ruined buildings, painted or incised on pottery, and discovered by archaeologists in sealed contexts are much easier to date and provide us with more secure evidence.

It was also during the Bronze Age, between 2000 and 1000 BC, that the Minoan and Mycenean cultures were building temples and palaces throughout Greece and the Aegean. One of the largest of these was excavated by Arthur Evens during the early 20th century, at Knossos on the island of Crete, the legendary location of the labyrinth in which King Minos

ABOVE *Many of the coins minted at the town of Knossos, on the island of Crete, during the 3rd to 1st centuries BC bear the labyrinth symbol on their reverse, in recognition of the location of the fabled home of the Minotaur.*

imprisoned the ferocious Minotaur – half man, half bull. It was here, according to the myths recorded by the earliest Greek writers, that Theseus fought and killed the Minotaur. Yet, surprisingly, no examples of the labyrinth symbol have been found at the labyrinth itself; the famous labyrinth coins from Knossos date from subsequent Hellenistic occupation of the site, a thousand years after the building had been destroyed. The Minoans and Myceneans were the first Europeans to produce written records of their trading transactions, recorded on sun-baked clay tablets inscribed with an archaic form of the Greek language known as Linear B (the earlier Linear A remains undeciphered). It is on one of these tablets from the palace of King Nestor at Pylos in southern Greece, actually preserved by the fire that destroyed the palace in c.1200 BC, that we have the earliest accurately dated example of the distinctive labyrinth symbol, the forerunner of all subsequent labyrinth and puzzle maze designs.

It is important to remember that these early labyrinths are not mazes in the sense that most people would think of today. There is only a single circuitous pathway that leads from the entrance to the central goal. Although the original use and purpose of these labyrinth designs remains conjectural, there is evidence that they were originally marked out on the ground and used as patterns for sacred dances and even as exercises for demonstrating skilful horse riding, but no such physical labyrinths have survived the ravages of time. We have only the depictions of the symbol itself, on artefacts that have survived by chance, to be discovered by modern researchers. Wherever they occur at this early time, and examples have been recorded throughout southern Europe, the Middle East and northern Africa, especially around the trading centres surrounding the Mediterranean Sea, the design employed is, almost without exception, exactly the same. How does this faithful reproduction of a complicated symbol occur across such a wide geographical and cultural area? Although the design might at first appear complex – and the archaeological record favours the survival of non-perishable materials – there is little evidence that the design was "written down" in order to facilitate its spread. Indeed, all the evidence points to the use of a "shorthand" transmission technique, whereby just the central core – a cross, angles, and dots – of the design is drawn first, and the remaining concentric circles are simply connected to the points around the central core of the design. Easily memorized, this technique has been passed on and used for over three thousand years. Such a trick of drawing skill, scratched in the dust with a stick can be passed to another, whatever language they might speak, and this was surely part of the appeal of this specific design, allowing it to survive unchanged and prosper for thousands of years in an essentially pre-literate world.

THE ROMAN EMPIRE AND CHRISTIAN ACCEPTANCE

The legend of Theseus and the Minotaur battling in the labyrinth was a great favourite with Roman writers and readers alike. With the story came the labyrinth symbol, and both became popular. A famous piece of graffiti scratched on a house at Pompeii, Italy, just before the town was buried by the eruption of Mount Vesuvius in AD 79, depicts the labyrinth alongside an inscription equating the owner of the house to the Minotaur. The labyrinth became a favourite theme for the design of mosaic pavements, as attested by more than 60 recorded examples discovered during excavations of Roman towns and villas from North Africa to northern England, and from Portugal to Cyprus. The central goals of these mosaic labyrinths were usually embellished with a decorative panel, often depicting some element from the story of Theseus and the Minotaur, and many are surrounded by representations of defensive

LEFT An illuminated manuscript produced during the late 12th century at Regensburg, southern Germany. At the centre of the labyrinth, Theseus battles with the Minotaur, as explained by the accompanying inscription.

RIGHT One of the best preserved and most elaborate of the Roman mosaic labyrinths. Produced in the late 3rd century AD, the central panel is occupied by Theseus fighting the Minotaur. Discovered in 1815 at Loig, near Salzburg, Austria, it is now on display at the Vienna Kunsthistorisches Museum.

RIGHT *The octagonal pavement labyrinth laid in black and white marble in the nave of the basilica at St. Quentin in northern France in 1495. Modelled on the similar labyrinth at nearby Amiens Cathedral, this is one of only a handful of original medieval pavement labyrinths to have survived.*

walls – surely an allusion to the order and security of Roman life. The location of a number of these mosaic labyrinths inside the entrances to civic and private buildings, even tombs, would suggest that the design was seen as a protective device, to confuse unwelcome visitors, whether from the real or spiritual world.

Study of these mosaic labyrinths reveals that new designs were developed during the first few centuries AD; they were increasingly complex and with a greater number of turns and circuits than before, and were more suited to exploit the space and effects provided by the medium of mosaic. These new designs were too complicated to be remembered by the mnemonic that had sufficed for the previous two millennia, and for the first time in labyrinth history, a written medium on which to record the designs was needed. Although no examples survive, contemporary writers record that mosaic designs were taken around the Roman Empire in copybooks, usually made of parchment or papyrus rolls. Most surprising, however, is the fact that practically all of these mosaic labyrinths had paths too narrow to actually walk – they were for decorative and contemplative purposes only.

The transition from a simple folk custom to an artistic design tradition, recognized from one end of the empire to the other, allowed the next important phase of labyrinth development to take place – the acceptance of the labyrinth into the symbolism of the early Christian Church. This is a surprising leap considering the clearly Pagan origins of the Theseus story so closely associated with the labyrinth.

The first evidence for this Christianization of the labyrinth comes from Roman Algeria, where a mosaic laid in the floor of the Christian basilica at Al-Asnam in AD 324 combines the familiar design of a square Roman labyrinth with a word-square spelling out "Sancta Eclesia" (Holy Church) occupying the central goal instead of Theseus and the Minotaur. Despite the decline of the Roman Empire, the fortune of the labyrinth in early Christian thinking prospered, and several prominent Christian philosophers employed the labyrinth as an

RIGHT *A small labyrinth set into the wall of Lucca Cathedral in northern Italy. Dating from the 12th century, this is one of the first examples of the medieval Christian labyrinth design to be found in an architectural setting. It is accompanied by an inscription explaining that this is the labyrinth that Daedalus built on the Greek island of Crete.*

allegory for the complexities of the matters under discussion. The pathway of the labyrinth, full of twists and turns but with no choices and ultimately leading to only one goal, was seen as symbolic of Christ's preordained life and of the tests of devotion presented to the faithful Christian. The concentric pathways surrounding the centre of the labyrinth were also equated with the early medieval view of the structure of the universe, Earth-centred and surrounded by the orbits of the Sun, Moon, and planets, based on the teachings of Plato and Ptolemy. This cosmological connection was especially important, for the labyrinth soon began to appear in manuscripts concerned with astronomical and computational tables designed for calculating the date of Easter – the subject of many dogmatic schisms in the early Church.

The majority of original manuscripts of these early Christian authors have long since been lost to war and vandalism, but copies of their works, produced in the scriptoriums of early Christian foundations and monasteries across Europe, kept many important texts in circulation. While the text was slavishly hand copied word for word onto vellum, the workers in the scriptoriums were able to append drawings and diagrams at key moments to further illustrate the author's point. A number of these surviving manuscripts from the 9th century AD onwards have labyrinths drawn in the margins or on the concluding page and these allow us to chart a number of further changes to the labyrinth designs in use at this time. The widespread adoption of a four-fold division of the labyrinth suggests a cross at the centre and a conscious attempt to Christianize an obviously Pagan symbol, although the use of the labyrinth to illustrate historical and topographical texts, often based on the works of earlier Greek and Roman authors, sometimes allows depictions of Theseus and his epic battle with the Minotaur once again to occupy the centre of the design. No doubt the parallels between this old Pagan myth and Christ's harrowing of the Devil in Hell were not lost on the authors and illustrators of these manuscripts.

CHURCHES AND CATHEDRALS

By the 12th century, one particular labyrinth form was in popular use in the manuscripts. This design has a distinctive four-fold symmetry with a pathway that sweeps back and forth through all regions of the design in a fashion that is both visually and mathematically satisfying. This was the "accepted" form for use in the church, with obvious Christian symbolism built into its structure; it soon started to appear in Italy as decorative carvings and floor mosaics, and in France where it was laid in tiles and coloured stone in the floors of churches and cathedrals. The most influential example from this time, constructed during the first decade of the 13th century and still surviving, spans the floor of the nave in Chartres Cathedral in northern France. Here, for the first time, we have labyrinths that were designed to be followed on foot, rather than by eye. It is reputed that these labyrinths were walked as substitutes for long pilgrimages after the enthusiasm of the Crusades had abated. Many are situated in cathedrals that were part of the network of pilgrimage routes that crisscrossed Europe during the medieval period. In many instances, they are situated just inside the entrance to the building, as if a reminder of the long journey that had brought the pilgrim to this spot. Their careful placement within the geometric layout of the cathedrals has been

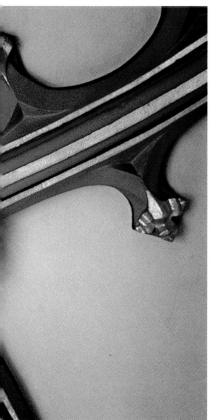

taken by modern writers to indicate that they contain a wealth of coded information concerning the construction of the cathedrals and other, more esoteric, matters. Although evidence is scant, there are records that provide clues to the purpose of these spectacular labyrinths and their meaning to the builders and clergy of the cathedrals.

Several of these labyrinths are recorded in contemporary documents as "Domus Dedalus" (The House of Daedalus), in reference to the builder of the Minotaur's prison, the original labyrinth on Crete. Medieval masons were fond of comparing their work to that of this great artificer from the Classical world. A few even had inlaid plaques with Theseus and the Minotaur shown – a curious piece of symbolism to be incorporated in the greatest celebrations of Christian teaching of their age. However, to have walked on a representation of Christ himself would have been sacrilege of the highest order. It is known that some of these cathedral labyrinths were the scenes of symbolic games and dances; a ball-game known as pelota was played at Easter by the clergy on the pavement labyrinth in Auxerre Cathedral, central France. The popularity of the labyrinth in this context, with its multiple layers of meaning and appeal for many levels of society, has provided a puzzle for modern scholars to explain. The labyrinth design symbolized the tortuous path that the good Christian followed towards redemption, both in everyday life and on pilgrimage. It would surely have been seen as illustrative of the pattern of Christ's life and inevitable fate, and in this role labyrinths continued to serve a contemplative purpose, an allegory of medieval Christian life.

LEFT *The Völudarhúsið (Wayland's House) stone labyrinth, situated amid the lava fields on the flanks of Snæfellsjökull volcano on the remote northwest coast of Iceland. It was probably first constructed from the 16th to 18th centuries by Norwegian fishermen from a nearby fishing station.*

Formerly widespread in France and Italy, with outlying examples recorded (but long since destroyed) in Germany and Poland, centuries of neglect and changes in church doctrine have resulted in the loss of many of these pavement labyrinths. The famed example in Chartres Cathedral, remains in good condition, although the central brass plaque was torn up at the time of the French Revolution. Unfortunately, today's visitors to the cathedral will often find the labyrinth covered in chairs. Other pavement labyrinths at St Quentin and Bayeux, also in France, and one in the town hall in Gent, Belgium, are similarly well preserved. The original labyrinth in Amiens Cathedral, nothern France, was destroyed in the early 19th century and only the central plaque survives; however, an exact replica was re-laid here in the 1890s. The early pavement labyrinths in Italy have fared less well – only fragments and smaller decorative stone carvings survive, although two late examples from the 16th century are preserved in the San Vitale basilica in Ravenna and in the Castel Sant' Angelo in Rome. In addition to these medieval pavement labyrinths and decorative carvings, there are others found in churches and cathedrals in France, the Netherlands, and England, although all of these date from the late 19th century, when architects were restoring old cathedrals and building new churches and chapels in imitation of the Gothic style. It is not surprising that, inspired by the cathedrals of France, labyrinths in these settings underwent a significant revival at this time, although for purely aesthetic reasons as the original purpose had long been forgotten.

Labyrinths in churches are also found throughout much of Scandinavia. A few are simple graffiti, but the majority are painted as wall or ceiling decoration, as frescos applied directly onto fresh plaster. Unlike the elaborate labyrinth designs in churches to the south, they are nearly all of the old "classical" design, or developments from it. Over 30 examples have now been recorded, with a number of new ones found in recent years, as church restoration projects removed centuries of lime-wash to reveal the original medieval wall paintings. They are scattered across southern Norway, Sweden, and Finland, with the largest concentration

in Denmark. In association with the extensive wall decorations of medieval churches in the region, it is likely that preachers would have pointed out the labyrinth designs to illustrate their sermons, but the exact role they played is unclear. All of these examples can be dated between the late 14th and early 16th centuries, with the possible exception of a unique labyrinth at Grinstad, in Dalsland, Sweden, which may belong to the early 13th century.

LABYRINTHS OF STONE AND TURF

In addition to the labyrinths on the walls of Scandinavian churches, stones and boulders were used to form the walls of labyrinths found throughout the Nordic countries of Sweden, Norway, and Finland. Found above the Arctic Circle and particularly around the shorelines of the Baltic Sea, these stone labyrinths are also known from Iceland, Arctic Russia, and Estonia; these outlying groups have probably originated from Nordic settlers or trading contacts.

Many of these Scandinavian stone labyrinths are found close to the coastline, and were certainly built by fishing communities during the medieval period, when labyrinths were also occasionally painted on the walls of churches in the south of the region. Recent advances in dating techniques have been applied to the stone labyrinths around the Baltic shoreline of Sweden, and it is now known that these labyrinths were constructed from the 13th century to modern times, with a notable peak in the 16th and 17th centuries. This was a period of

extensive colonization of the area by Swedish settlers and fishing fleets. Many are situated adjacent to natural harbours and old seasonal fishing dwellings where fish would have been dried and salted during the arctic summer. One can certainly imagine that the local children would have played in these labyrinths while the fishing parties worked. A cluster of these stone labyrinths in arctic Norway is associated with ancient Saami burial grounds; a similar link is found with stone labyrinths on remote islands in the White Sea in Arctic Russia.

A fascinating group in southern Sweden, found far inland high up in the hills, is associated with ancient grave fields used from the Bronze Age through to the Viking period. These labyrinths may have been connected with pagan practices, where the labyrinth was seen as the abode of the spirits of the ancestors, but yet no dating technique has been developed to confirm their age – the mounds of stones and boulders piled up for grave cairns would have provided adequate building material for the labyrinths at any time. Although we can only guess at the rituals carried out at these ancient grave-field labyrinths, the uses of the coastal labyrinths are better known from both folklore and eye-witness accounts. Until the early 20th century, fishermen would walk the labyrinths before putting to sea to ensure good catches and bring favourable weather – unwelcome winds would become trapped in the circuitous coils of the labyrinth. In Finland, the Lapp hunters and shepherds would walk the labyrinths to protect themselves from wolves and wolverines and to entrap the trolls and other evil spirits, who would follow them in but be unable to escape.

The popularity of the labyrinth in Scandinavia was quite remarkable. Some 500 or more of these stone labyrinths have been recorded in the region, and the symbol also occurs occasionally as carvings on wooden household objects. As with the labyrinths in Scandinavian

LEFT A simple hedge maze appears in the background of this painting of the story of David and Bathsheba, executed by Henri met de Bles in Antwerp during the 1540s. Although depicting mythical scenes, such paintings and prints often provide record of the early hedge maze designs current at the time.

LEFT Completed in 1721, the hedge maze built by the Pisani family at the Villa Pisani, near Padua in Italy, is a rare survivor from the period. More complicated than the earlier hedge mazes, this example was further embellished with a central tower boasting a spiral staircase to view the maze upon completion.

LEFT *Cut in 1660, as commemorated on the central pillar, the turf labyrinth on the village green at Hilton in eastern England is still beautifully maintained. It is typical of the public labyrinths that were especially popular in Britain and Germany during the 16th and 17th centuries.*

churches, the stone labyrinths of northern Europe are predominantly of the earliest "classical" type, or simple derivations from it. In a mobile society where books were rare, the labyrinth was once again transmitted by means of the ancient mnemonic technique. These stone labyrinths were extremely long lasting, and many of them still survive, especially in remote areas and on offshore islands.

Turf labyrinths, or "turf mazes" as they are popularly known, were once found throughout Britain, the old Germanic Empire (including modern Poland and the Czech Republic), Denmark, and southern Sweden. Formed by cutting away the ground surface to leave turf ridges and shallow trenches, the convoluted pattern produces a single pathway leading to the centre of the design. In some examples, a small mound stands at the goal, while embankments surround others. Usually circular, although sometimes square or polygonal, the designs employed are a curious mixture of ancient "classical" types, found throughout the area, and the medieval Christian types, found principally in England.

A number of interesting variants of both types are found among the 30 or so examples with plans recorded. Some of these are clearly original developments on the design theme – a number in northern Germany and Poland replace the central region of a classical labyrinth with a double spiral to produce a quick exit path, ideally suited for processional dances. Others show a number of decorative developments and the outcome of errors generated by inaccurate re-cuttings, presumably when part or all of the design becomes obscured by wear or neglect. Turf labyrinths, by nature of their living medium, are soon overgrown and lost, if routine repair and re-cutting is not carried out. In many villages this was performed regularly, often in connection with fairs or religious festivals, particularly around Easter and Whitsun.

Although around 50 examples are documented, and several hundred sites have been postulated from place-name evidence, only eleven historic turf labyrinths survive – eight in England and three in Germany. Although turf-cut labyrinths are mentioned by the Roman writer Pliny in his *Historia Naturalis*, most of those recorded certainly date from the medieval

period or later. Folklore and the few contemporary records that survive suggest that they were a popular feature of fairs and other festivities. Many are found on village greens or commons, often near churches, but sometimes they are sited on hilltops or more remote locations.

THE ORIGINS OF GARDEN MAZES

It was during the late medieval period that labyrinths found their way into the gardens of the nobility, and for the first time there is evidence that the designs employed take the next major step in the story – the transformation from labyrinths into puzzle mazes formed of hedges. Ironically, the first positive evidence for a hedge maze is the record of the destruction of an example in Paris in 1431. However, it is clear that the concept was familiar c.1450, when an anonymous English author penned *The Assembly of Ladies*, a poem describing a low hedge maze and the efforts of a group of ladies to reach the centre. Surely this was a maze with a choice of pathways, or there would be no confusion about the correct path to take. However, it is not until the early 1500s, with the widespread advent of printing in Europe, that there are the first indications of the designs employed for these early garden mazes and labyrinths.

Unlike the flat, essentially two-dimensional, church and turf labyrinths, where a choice of pathway is hardly ever encountered – and indeed, is pointless if the course of the paths can be followed by eye – the use of three-dimensional hedging materials allowed multi-path mazes to be developed from single-path labyrinths. However, the surprising feature of early depictions of hedge mazes is that many of them are in fact unicursal labyrinths. At best they are rarely more than simple adaptations of the widespread medieval labyrinth designs.

BELOW *Probably the most famous hedge maze in the world, and certainly one of the oldest, the maze at Hampton Court Palace in England was originally planted in 1690. The design has been extensively copied and adapted for hedge mazes (and other forms) as far away as the United States of America and Australia.*

Many of the earlier garden labyrinths were influenced by classical reference and designed for contemplative exercise of both mind and body, but later examples increasingly developed as places of gentle entertainment, somewhere to dally and engage in conversation, and with the inclusion of shaded bowers and other features, a site for romance. A number of paintings from the early 16th century onwards depict labyrinths and simple mazes with low hedges, tunnels, and arbours; couples are often shown strolling around the paths. With full-height hedges and more complex designs, they soon became a puzzle and a challenge, and an increasingly popular feature in gardens across Europe.

During the period from 1550 to 1650, a number of influential hedge mazes were built from Italy across to Spain, up through France, Germany, and the Low Countries to Britain. The advent of a number of early books on garden practice soon disseminated new ideas and, more importantly, original designs for garden mazes to a wide audience. Well known among these was *Libri cinque d'architettura* by Sebastiano Serlio, first published in Italy in 1537; this book includes plans for two labyrinths, subsequently planted during the following decades as hedge mazes in gardens throughout Italy, France, and Britain. Interestingly, the same plans would also seem to have been employed for pavement labyrinths in Ravenna and Rome (*see p.27*). The engravings of garden maze designs produced by Hans Vredeman de Vries and Hans Puec in Antwerp during the 1580s and 1590s show simple mazes, and even true labyrinths, formed from low turf ridges that fit easily among the *parterre* garden layouts of the period. Thomas Hyll's *The Gardener's Labyrinth*, first published in London in the 1560s, also influenced a number of garden mazes, and his designs were used for several of the later turf labyrinths, including the surviving example at Saffron Walden in Essex, eastern England. With designs for garden mazes freely available, they soon spread from the gardens of villas and castles to modest gardens. Unfortunately, none of these early garden mazes still exist, although paintings and engravings recording their plans survive, and in recent years have provided inspiration for several authentic re-creations in period settings.

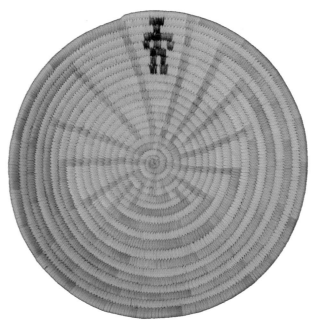

LEFT *In the Victorian period artists and architects left Britain to travel around the world. They returned with ideas and designs for projects at home. This beautiful gilded labyrinth in the Watts Chapel at Compton in Surrey, southeast England, is based on a design from Ravenna in Italy. Four more labyrinths appear on roof corbels on the exterior of the building.*

LEFT *A woven basket produced in modern times by the Pima peoples of southern Arizona, US. The design, popularly known as "The Man in the Maze," represents the passageway that leads into the home of the founder of the tribe. It is identical to the "classical" labyrinths found throughout Europe and Asia.*

Hedge mazes carried on flourishing and developing during the late 17th and 18th centuries. The popular earlier designs continued to be repeated, and increasingly grandiose elaborative, decorative, and complex designs began to appear. The famous example from Hampton Court Palace (*see p.34*), is probably the best-known and oldest true survivor from this period, but other hedge mazes from the early 18th century live on in France, Denmark, and Italy. They also spread during this time into Scandinavia, across to Prague and Moravia, and even as far as China. A splendid garden maze, constructed with high brick walls and containing small groves of trees and a central pavilion, was built in the gardens of the Imperial Court at Peking, c.1766, but was regrettably destroyed in 1860 (*see p.35*).

LABYRINTHS IN OTHER LANDS

Colonial influences took hedge mazes to the US, India, Australia, and New Zealand. However, the simple labyrinth design had already reached a number of these places long before European adventurers set foot on those distant shores. Rocks engraved with the labyrinth symbol have been found in India and Pakistan dating back two thousand years, and the design is widespread in India in the form of labyrinths built with boulders (just as in Scandinavia), temple carvings, and paintings, even as tattoo designs. From here the labyrinth travelled to Indonesia, reaching as far as Java and it is still in popular use among the Batak peoples of Sumatra. But perhaps the biggest surprise is the presence of the labyrinth symbol in the Americas. In widespread use as a symbol for the abode of their ancestors among the desert-dwelling native peoples of the American Southwest, the labyrinth has also been reported from as far afield as Ecuador and Brazil. It is often difficult, however, to provide any accurate dating for most of the labyrinth-inscribed rock panels and artefacts from these regions, and it currently remains unclear whether the labyrinth was introduced to the native people of the Americas by early Spanish colonizers, or was discovered quite independently.

TRADITIONAL MAZES

The traditional maze, formed of closely clipped and tangled living hedges, is for most people the archetypal form; indeed, it is often the only type of maze they expect to find in a formal garden. A long-established tradition throughout much of Europe, the hedge maze has found homes in gardens around the world and now, at the beginning of the 21st century, it is once again enjoying a wave of popularity with innovative original designs and features to enchant a new generation of visitors.

PRESERVING THE PAST

Mazes formed from tangled living hedges have been a feature of the gardens and parks of royalty, the rich, and the well-to-do for at least six hundred years. The first hedge mazes were planted during the late medieval and early Renaissance periods. During the 16th and 17th centuries gardening writers and advisors recommended them as essential elements of any well-executed garden designs and consequently they appeared in gardens across Europe. Although most early hedge mazes have long since disappeared, contemporary documents, engravings, and plans of the estates and gardens often preserve details of their former mazes. These not only supply evidence for the existence and development of early hedge mazes, but they have also provided valuable design information for authentic restorations.

APELDOORN.
Dwaaltuin b d.
Julianatoren.

PREVIOUS PAGES *With paths bounded by swirling, spiralling hedges, Greg Bright's design for the hedge maze at Longleat House, Wiltshire, southwest England, was to prove immensely influential and a major turning point in the fortunes of this most traditional form of maze.*

LEFT *A postcard from the 1920s records the original plan of the hedge maze in the Koningin Julianatoren entertainment park at Apeldoorn in the Netherlands. Planted in 1916, it is the model of a well-tended maze.*

LEFT *A recent aerial photograph of the Koningin Julianatoren maze illustrates the problems that can arise when a hedge maze suffers neglect. Less than half of the 1916 maze now survives (see above), although the original pattern can still be discerned. It now provides a backdrop to more modern attractions.*

ABOVE *The hornbeam hedge maze in the grounds of Egeskov Castle, on the island of Fyn in Denmark, was probably planted in the early 18th century and is certainly the oldest hedge maze in that country. The pathway is a rectangular version of the design at Hampton Court Palace in England.*

However, the ownership and upkeep of a hedge maze is not without its own particular problems. Trimming the hedges regularly throughout the growing season and watering well during dry spells are just the start. All hedge mazes are prone to the damage caused by visitors who either become frustrated by the puzzle or impatient to reach the centre; gaps forced between the stems of individual plants are soon widened and can prove difficult to repair. Replacing sections of the hedge that die off can be particularly troublesome, especially when the maze is in a public setting. The small handful of historic hedge mazes that have survived the passage of time show well the various trials and tribulations that beset the existence of these mazes, constructed as they are of a living, growing material.

The maze at Hampton Court Palace, originally planted c.1690 for William III, now receives hundreds of thousands of visitors each year. The consequential wear and tear to the original yew hedges has necessitated a number of "patches" over the years. The use of different varieties of plants has resulted in uneven growth, and there is talk of a complete re-plant of the maze in the near future to address the current maintenance problems. The hedge maze at Egeskov Castle in Denmark, planted in the early 1700s, still survives in pristine condition, due to diligent care and more modest visitor numbers.

The hedge maze at Staverden in the Netherlands, although first planted as recently as 1907, employs a design originally intended for a much larger ground area, with wide pathways for easy strolling and space for fountains and statuary within its walls. Confined to

an area of only 35 x 18m (116 x 59ft), the resulting narrow pathways are difficult to negotiate and easily become blocked by vigorous new growth. Impatient walkers have forced shortcuts through the hedges at a number of points and, unfortunately, the gardeners have then incorporated these into the design. In the same country, the huge hedge maze at Ruurlo has been more fortunate. Originally planted in 1890, it underwent extensive restoration in 1985 and, along with similarly fine examples at Menkemaborg and Het Oude Loo, form part of the remarkable collection of some 25 hedge mazes to be found in the Netherlands.

The survival of historic hedge mazes is often more a matter of chance than any process that favours the preservation of the most important or exciting examples. Fortunately, there is a selection of such historic mazes throughout Europe. In Italy, the mazes at the Villa Barbarigo in Vansanzibio and the Villa Pisani at Stra, near Padua (*see p.44*), are celebrated survivors from the many hedge mazes that once graced the gardens of villas throughout the country. The gardens at the Laberint d'Horta Park in Barcelona, Spain, were originally planted by the Marquis of Alfarràs from 1791 but they were restored towards the end of the 20th century. Central to the layout of the garden is a splendid hedge maze formed of fragrant clipped cypress trees, enhanced with statues and fountains with a decorated grotto at the goal. Now in excellent condition once again, this is without doubt one of the most attractive and enticing mazes in Europe. The hedge maze at Altjessnitz in Sachsen-Anhalt, northern Germany, originally planted c.1750, still survives in good condition, although the castle in whose grounds it formerly stood has long since been destroyed. The remarkable swirling

The hedge maze in the gardens of Hever Castle, Kent, southeast England, presents an image of the quintessential traditional hedge maze – its impact is even greater when cloaked in snow. William Waldorf Astor planted the maze in 1904 as part of his restoration of the castle and grounds. It is based on an old design assumed to be by Gervase Markham, first published in 1623 in Certaine excellent and new invented Knots and Mazes.

pathways of the laurel hedge maze at Glendurgan House in Cornwall, southwest England (*see pp.46–8*), were planted in 1833, and are now cared for by the National Trust.

While there may have been something of a decline in the popularity of garden mazes in Europe in the late 18th and early 19th centuries, an important development at this time had far-reaching consequences for the future of maze design, although it was not for another one hundred and fifty years that it became fully noticed and implemented. In the 1820s, Earl Stanhope, an eminent mathematician, designed at least three hedge mazes, including the surviving example at Chevening House, Kent, southeast England. These mazes represent the first serious application of mathematics and map theory to the design of mazes. Stanhope recognized that most mazes could be solved by the "hand-on-wall method" (that is, by always turning in the same direction), because the vast majority of previous maze designs, although containing multiple pathways, effectively only consisted of a single wall, albeit with numerous branches, surrounding those pathways. Stacked within a perimeter hedge, Stanhope's mazes contained a number of totally discrete sections of hedge, which, importantly, are not in contact with the goal at the centre. This not only makes a maze that is more difficult to solve, but with careful design skills, one that contains few dead ends along the way, producing a more fluid and less frustrating walking experience for the visitor. These are important factors in modern maze design, although they were little appreciated at the time.

The Italianate gardening style popular in Britain from c.1830–50 created several interesting maze designs, of which the recently restored yew maze in Bridge End Gardens in

ABOVE *Once a common feature in the gardens of Italian villas, only a handful of preserved specimens survive. This splendid example in the gardens of the Villa Pisani at Stra, near Padua, Italy, was planted in 1721 and features a tower with an external spiral staircase at its centre.*

Saffron Walden, and the splendid Somerleyton Hall maze near Lowestoft, both in eastern England, survive. The establishment of recreation grounds, pleasure gardens, and public parks during this time also provided a number of new opportunities for the planting of hedge mazes across Europe. From the mid-1800s until the outbreak of World War I in 1914 mazes as playgrounds for children, as well as places for dalliance by young lovers, were standard features of many well-designed public places. Although the designs employed are often little more than replicas or adaptations of old favourites, a fair number of these examples survive, including some restored in recent years as civic regeneration programs repair overgrown and neglected town and city gardens back to their former glory.

COLONIAL INFLUENCES

In the mid 19th century hedge mazes began to be exported to the far-flung colonies of the European sea-faring nations, especially those of the British Empire. They appeared in public, civic, and governmental parks and gardens as far away as Sierra Leone, India, and Australia. The first recorded example in Australia, planted in the Botanical Gardens at Ballarat, Victoria, in 1862, was replanted in the late 1880s and survived until 1954, although plans remain on

BELOW *The Laberint d'Horta Park in Barcelona, Spain, covers a total area of 8ha (20 acres) with a beautiful hedge maze at the centre. Money acquired during the 1990s as a grant from the European Union has allowed the gardens and the maze to be fully restored to the original layout, as conceived by the Marquis of Alfarràs in 1791.*

file to restore it again at sometime in the future. In New Zealand, the first hedge maze was planted in the Botanic Gardens at Dunedin in 1911. This too has now been destroyed. The designs of these colonial hedge mazes were rarely adventurous; many continued to use adaptations of the Hampton Court design, although the designers often faced the challenge of employing native plant species, better suited to the climate.

It was also during this period that hedge mazes came to the Americas. Surprisingly, the first recorded example, built at Harmony, Pennsylvania, c.1815, was in fact a hedge labyrinth, with just a single pathway leading to the centre. The Harmonists, a group of religious dissidents, exiled from their native Germany, established three communities in Pennsylvania and Indiana between 1805 and 1825, and built a labyrinth at each settlement to symbolize their spiritual quest. All the original labyrinths have been destroyed, although a reconstruction of one of them, planted in 1941 at the former Harmonist village of New Harmony, Indiana, has ironically taken the original labyrinth design, and with the addition of a few breaks in the walls, converted the design into a maze. The hedge mazes planted in America during the late 19th and early 20th centuries in the parks of major cities and popular coastal resorts alike have all perished. The hedge maze in the garden of the Governor's Palace at colonial Williamsburg, Virginia, was planted in 1935 and is one of the oldest surviving hedge mazes in America.

RECENT REVIVAL

While the hedge mazes of 19th-century parks and pleasure gardens were designed primarily to provide gentle entertainment and exercise, the international boom in tourism in the late 20th century has imposed new demands on the surviving historic hedge mazes. Never

ABOVE *The simple hedge maze at New Harmony in Indiana, was planted in 1941 to a plan adapted from a drawing of the original maze created in the town c.1815. Although one of the first such mazes planted in America, the original design was a single-path labyrinth, not a maze as such.*

PREVIOUS PAGES *The looping paths of the hedge maze in Glendurgan Gardens in Cornwall, southwest England, follow the contours of the sloping side of the valley on which it is situated. Planted with laurel hedges in 1833, it provides an interesting contrast to the regular, geometric mazes commonly planted at this time.*

designed for a continuous stream of feet, increased visitor numbers can significantly amplify wear and tear. Despite these problems, since the late 1970s there has been a dramatic revival of interest in the form, and the traditional hedge mazes are flourishing. Two distinct branches appear to have developed. While some new mazes have been built along familiar lines to provide a time-honoured element for themed or period installations in the grounds of stately houses and children's playparks alike, more adventurous designers have been experimenting with hedge mazes that stretch the boundaries of a medium that many commentators assumed was stuck in the past.

Pinning down the precise starting point of the current resurgence of mazes and labyrinths is by no means straightforward, but the planting of the enormous hedge maze at Longleat House in Wiltshire, England (*see pp.50–51*), in 1975 can be cited as a major turning point. Opened in 1978 and commissioned by Lord Weymouth (now the Marquis of Bath) to add a further attraction to the safari park, that had already put the stately house on the tourist map, the maze was designed by Greg Bright. His innovative swirling design, with complex spiralling pathways to disorient walkers, as well as bridges to link self-enclosed sections of the maze, proved an instant hit with visitors and, more importantly, demonstrated to those cynics convinced that mazes had had their day as visitor attractions, that there were

LEFT *The holly maze at Williamsburg in Virginia, was originally planted in 1935 to add an air of authenticity to the gardens of the Governor's House in the preserved colonial period town. The design of the maze is based closely on the celebrated example at Hampton Court Palace. At the time of writing this holly maze is undergoing a complete restoration.*

still new twists to be explored. The maze at Longleat entered the record books as the largest maze in the world. Others could claim larger overall dimensions, but Bright's maze at Longleat packed far more path length and complexity within its walls. Although the record was broken with the introduction of the truly huge wooden panel mazes in Japan in the mid-1980s, and then again by the maize mazes that have sprung up across the cornfields of America, Europe, and the far East since the mid-1990s, Longleat remains one of the most challenging hedge mazes in the world. Since 1994, the Marquis of Bath has added a further four mazes to his collection – two more hedge mazes with deeply symbolic designs made by Randoll Coate, a rose garden maze designed by Graham Burgess, and a mirror maze created by Adrian Fisher. Without doubt, the mazes at Longleat House now form one of the most impressive collections anywhere in Europe.

Many architects and designers have turned their hands to mazes since the early 1980s, but foremost among the designers of modern hedge mazes must surely be Adrian Fisher. Since building his first maze in his father's garden in southern England in 1975, and becoming a full-time maze designer in the early 1980s, Fisher has built over 300 mazes worldwide. Early partnerships with Coate, Burgess, and others, brought a number of different influences and design themes to Fisher's work, which has developed to introduce radical new interactive features and construction materials to the maze-design world. Working with an impressive variety of materials, including mirrors, wooden fencing panels, brick pavement, coloured plastic tiles, and walls of water fountains, he brings his love of mathematics and three-dimensional space, coupled with an acute business sense, to his vocation of designing and creating unique and beautiful mazes. Although better known for his pioneering designs for maize mazes and complex mathematical mazes, Fisher has also successfully turned his hand to the more traditional hedge mazes, with a number of installations at premier tourist sites in Britain, other European countries, and further afield.

Especially notable among Fisher's hedge mazes is the dramatic example at Leeds Castle in Kent, southeast England, constructed in 1988 in partnership with Coate and Vernon Gibberd. The hedge maze itself features an entertaining design with a "castellated"

ABOVE *The hedge maze in the grounds of Longleat House in Wiltshire, southwest England, was first opened to the public in 1978 and proved an instant attraction. Covering an area of 114 x 53m (380 x 175ft), it challenged many perceptions of the nature of hedge mazes and was to prove instrumental in the current revival of interest in the form.*

RIGHT *The spiralling pathways and lack of any rectangular grid within the Longleat maze make it difficult to navigate. Any perception of left or right or your exact whereabouts in the design soon break down. Coupled with the enormous scale of the layout, this is truly a complex maze to solve and at least an hour should be allowed to reach the centre.*

perimeter hedge, originally planted between twin rows of green wooden trellis work – an imaginative solution to the problem of opening a hedge maze to the public before the hedges have gained full height and thickness. The goal of the maze is clearly indicated by a stone tower at the centre. However, the ramp that leads to the top of the tower reveals the extraordinary feature that marks this maze out from all the rest. Beneath the tower is a dramatic underground shell-lined grotto with running water features, modelled on similar features from Renaissance gardens; the grotto runs beneath the maze and exits beside the entrance. For the maze walker this provides both a wonderful reward for accepting the maze's challenge and a quick exit from the maze without the need to retrace the path. For the owner it provides a means to dramatically improve visitor-flow numbers at peak times.

Opened in May 1992, Fisher's gigantic hedge maze at Drielandenpunt (Three Lands Point) in the Netherlands is situated where the Dutch, Belgium, and German borders meet.

The maze is 90m (295ft) in diameter and has nine rows of foaming fountains that block the pathways, rising and falling according to the movement of the visitors, an innovation that introduces an additional time-and-direction related factor to the puzzle of the maze. Three large wooden bridges and a central tower within the maze, as well as a sheltered courtyard with refreshments and a puzzle shop, have ensured that this maze is now the most popular in the Netherlands, and at the time of writing has around 130,000 visitors a year. Fisher's bold design of three interlocking heraldic beasts from each of the three countries' national flags, while discernable from the central tower, is best appreciated from the air. Such aerial images provide eye-catching publicity for the maze and logos for souvenirs; they also create "product identity," essential for a stand-alone maze attraction, in a market where most tourist orientated mazes are adjunct to existing and long-established attractions. At Edinburgh Zoo, Scotland, a more recent installation, designed by Fisher in 1995, and in the shape of a turtle, has a number of interactive features designed to illustrate Darwin's Theory of Evolution. Water jets, this time controlled by electronic testers that determine certain characteristics of the walker, block pathways that either allow further access or return the walker to the start to "evolve" further. It is certain that Fisher and other modern designers will continue to develop the principles, materials, and designs for hedge mazes, wherever these mazes are planted.

RESTORATION PROJECTS

The closing decades of the 20th century saw not only a remarkable revival of fortunes for new and innovative hedge mazes, but also a much-needed appreciation of the importance of mazes as an integral part of historic garden designs. The study of garden history has gone hand-in-hand with a number of projects to restore key historic gardens to their former glory after years of neglect and misunderstanding. Inevitably, some important hedge mazes have been rescued from states of terminal overgrowth or replanted from archival plans. Additionally, several re-creations of period gardens in the grounds of contemporary houses and palaces have taken old engravings for inspiration, and suitable garden mazes have been added to the finished layout to provoke an atmospheric surrounding. A notable example planted with dwarf box in the Tudor garden of Hatfield House in Hertfordshire, southern England, is based on designs found in 16th-century prints; it makes a wonderful re-creation of an otherwise completely lost class of maze, in a splendidly authentic setting, to compliment the full height yew hedge maze planted in 1840. A similar re-created maze, although this time just cut into turf, in the garden of Chenies Manor, Hertfordshire, also in southern England, is based on a maze in the background of a 1573 painting of a former owner of the house. In the late 1990s, a hedge maze was added to the gardens at Villandry, in northern France, likewise based on period designs, and a sure sign that further examples of this genre can be expected in historic garden re-creations in the future.

The recent trend for restoration of overgrown or lost hedge mazes has produced several notable success stories. A pioneering project to restore a small yew hedge maze in Bridge End

LEFT *Seemingly deep underground, the shell-lined grotto 6m (20ft) beneath the centre of the Leeds Castle maze in Kent, southeast England, provides an unexpected reward for the diligent visitor. It also links to the exit tunnel that returns to the start, so there is no need to retrace the path. This dramatic conclusion to the maze further challenges the perception of how a maze should "work."*

LEFT *Above ground, the Leeds Castle maze resembles any other hedge maze, but the stone tower at the centre hides the secret that marks this example out from the competition. The maze was designed by Adrian Fisher, Randoll Coate, and Vernon Gibberd, and opened to the public in 1988.*

Gardens in the town of Saffron Walden (justly famous for its turf labyrinth on the nearby town common) in Essex, eastern England, set an impressive precedent for detailed recording and careful restoration on a limited budget. Tony Collins and John Bosworth, two local council officers, working since 1980 on a plan for the restoration of the late 18th- and early 19th-century town garden, first turned their attention to the chronically overgrown hedge maze in 1982. After thorough surveys of the maze, it was concluded that the original yew bushes – now trees – were unlikely to regenerate if cut back hard, so a decision was taken to uproot the bushes and replant. This allowed an archaeological investigation of the site to be carried out, which revealed a number of important finds connected with the life of the maze and enabled previous occupation evidence from the site to be recorded. Sections taken from the trunks of the yew trees proved that the maze was planted in either 1838 or 1839. Following careful consultation of existing plans, old photographs, and the visible remains of the ground plan, the maze was replanted in 1984 and at the beginning of the 21st century it is once again looking splendid. A replica of the original central-viewing platform installed in 2000 provides the visitor with views across the maze and the adjacent gardens.

A similar project to restore an important 18th-century formal walled garden at Castle Bromwich Hall, near Birmingham, in the Midlands, England, followed essentially similar lines and showed that the overgrown holly hedge maze in the grounds was first planted c.1870. Likewise, the original holly planting was too overgrown to save, and a complete replant in 1989 has now restored this maze to its former glory and swollen the ranks of the surviving historic hedge mazes. Both of these projects relied heavily on volunteer workers and financial donations, but show admirably the standard of work that can be achieved in these circumstances.

BELOW With hedges only 7–10cm (2½–4in) high, the box maze in the re-created Tudor garden at Hatfield House in England is based on 16th-century engravings of contemporary gardens. It provides an atmospheric re-construction of an early form of traditional hedge maze that is now completely lost.

More than eight million visitors a year enjoy the beauty of the Schönbrunn Palace Gardens, near Vienna, northeast Austria, although few would have been aware that the gardens formerly possessed a huge hedge maze, first planted c. 1750, consisting of a number of separate mazes linked together. Gradually the maze decayed – by 1865 less than half remained and by the early years of the 20th century little survived of the 18th-century maze, even though the original ground plan was still outlined by the shapes of the re-planted areas that now occupied the area. During the late 1990s, restoration work in the gardens saw one quarter of the maze restored in its original location, although the design was subtly altered to provide a new entrance point.

With a history that stretches some six hundred years, and surviving examples that are over three hundred years old, the traditional hedge maze has proved to be a resilient and adaptable form, ever able to meet the challenge of a new generation of owners and visitors. Undoubtedly, in the future further hedge mazes will be restored and re-created to join the increasingly diverse modern examples. With interest in historic gardens currently booming, the provision of an entertaining diversion in a beautiful garden setting has ensured that the hedge will continue to exercise its spell in the 21st century, just as effectively as it did in the gardens of the medieval and Renaissance periods.

MODERN MATERIALS

The modern tourist industry has kindled a revival of interest in mazes, but the pressure of seeing an immediate return on investment demands that mazes built today must be ready to receive paying visitors tomorrow. No longer can the prospective maze owner be prepared to wait while their maze grows to full height. Instead, today's maze designers have taken on the challenge of using modern materials and techniques to provide instant amazement for those wishing to indulge in the craze for mazes.

MAIZE MAZES

The latest maze craze to grip the imagination of the public and media alike is that for the maize mazes that have been grown in cornfields across the US and Europe since the early 1990s. The expansion of maize mazes has paralleled the media frenzy that surrounds the mysterious "crop-circles" that appear each summer in the wheat fields of southern England and elsewhere in Europe. The first maize maze was made in 1993 by Adrian Fisher and Don Frantz at Annville, Pennsylvania, in the shape of a giant stegosaurus, for a Red Cross fund-raising event. While traditional hedge mazes can take years to grow to a suitable height, the extraordinary growth rate of this annual crop, coupled with the strength of its stems and the linear planting patterns of modern farm machinery, makes this an ideal medium for the maze creator to exploit – albeit one that is doomed to wither and die at the end of the summer.

While a few examples, such as the "Labyrinthus" attraction at Reignac-sur-Indre (*see above*), are planted to a pre-described pattern on the same roadside plot each year, most maize mazes are designed to fit whatever field is available. Created by removing rows

ABOVE *The "Labyrinthus" cornfield maze at Reignac-sur-Indre, Touraine, near Tours in France. First opened in 1997, this maze is replanted each year with a different plan and theme, and covers a total area of 12ha (30 acres) with 8km (5 miles) of pathways.*

of plants, the large and often complex designs employed provide both a satisfying puzzle for the walker and striking opportunities for aerial photography. Such media-friendly images have proved popular with newspapers and television alike, and the resulting publicity has allowed some of these maize mazes to attract over 50,000 paying visitors during their two-to-three-month life span. Attracting visitors to adjacent farm produce outlets provides a great incentive for farmers – an annual maze in Petaluma, California, draws thousands to solve the maze and buy their Halloween pumpkins at the same time. A number of such roadside mazes spring up each year, often with simple designs, but the production of dramatic looking mazes, guaranteed to catch the all-important eye of aerial photographers, and newspaper and television editors, has become an art-form.

Foremost among the designers is the redoubtable Adrian Fisher. Each year since 1993, Fisher's design team has produced an ever-increasing number of maize mazes at locations across Britain, Europe, North America, and Australia, with a different theme every year for the designs and marketing. Aimed at families, each maze has a number of additional puzzles to solve along the way, wooden bridges to provide viewpoints across the maze, sound systems, and even portable toilet facilities. While success always breeds imitation, and a number of other designers have entered the maize maze field in recent years, Fisher's mazes continue to give new, innovative features year after year, and his designs always receive good media and web coverage, as well as publication and merchandizing spin-offs. Laying out these huge mazes involves complex mathematical and geometric calculation based on the planting pattern of the maize itself. Several designers in the US have now started to use the GPS (Global Positioning Satellite) system to aid them with the initial layout in the otherwise featureless open fields.

From the outset, these maize mazes have been designed with an eye to capturing the Guinness World Record for the largest maze in history, and each year new contenders come forward to claim the prize – path lengths in excess of 6.5km (4 miles) are now

LEFT *Reaching over 2m (6½ft) high, the stems of the maize plants left standing between the pathways of a maize maze provide a dense, impenetrable barrier that requires little or no maintenance during the single season life span of the maze.*

PREVIOUS PAGES

Formed from hundreds of interlocking fence panels, the fashion for huge wooden panel mazes that swept Japan in the mid 1980s was, without doubt, the most remarkable of the modern maze crazes. Quick construction and instant visitor revenue were important factors in their popularity with developers.

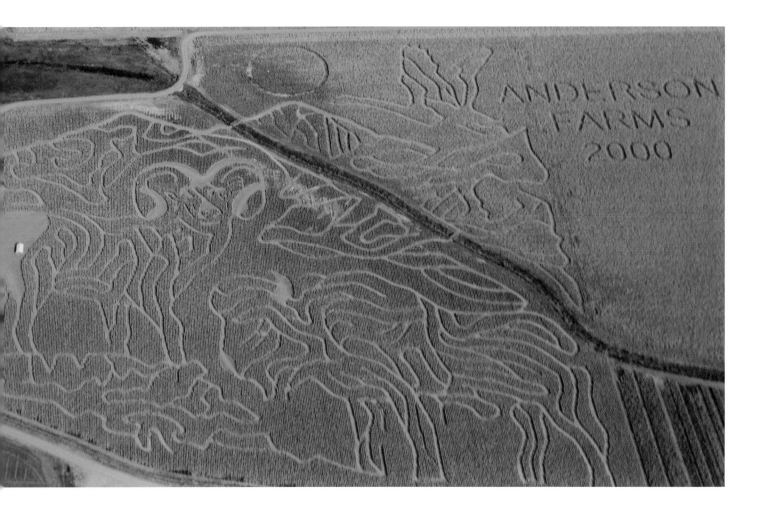

commonplace – but a point is reached where the path can become a chore, no longer a pleasure. Providing an enjoyable experience is always the aim for any designer of a puzzle maze hoping to appeal to a wide, family-based market.

MIRROR MAZES

Unlike the newly sprouted maize mazes, mirror mazes have been around since the late 19th century. Once a popular feature of seaside resorts, shows, and funfairs, in Europe and America alike, their fortunes waned as tastes in entertainment changed. An historic example at Lucerne in Switzerland (*see p.62*) is a rare survivor from those times, although rudimentary mirror mazes can still be found from time to time among the attractions at travelling fairs and circuses. The simple effect of multiple reflections and apparently endless pathways, which in fact lead nowhere, would seem to offer little real potential for modern maze designers, forever condemning them to a life on the road looking for another customer; however modern technology has sparked a dramatic revival for mirror mazes. New mazes are appearing annually at some of the most prestigious visitor attractions in Europe and America, and each new mirror maze adds a novel twist to an old idea that many had thought had seen its day. As with the maize mazes, the leading designer of this new generation of mirror mazes is Adrian Fisher, without doubt the most prolific maze designer in the world today.

ABOVE *With over 10km (6 miles) of pathways, this maize maze formed during the summer of 2000 at Erie, Colorado, employs a free-form construction technique where a meandering pathway produces a design only truly appreciable from the air.*

The perfection of modern glass production has been harnessed to produce large distortion-free mirrors ideally suited for the perfect angular alignment needed to create the flawless impression of endless corridors and chambers. Clever mathematical analysis of the effects possible with different settings of the mirrored panels has eliminated the feeling of being in a corridor effect that characterized traditional mirror mazes. Coupling the hardware with computerized lighting and sound effects now enhances the sensual deception beyond the merely visual illusions previously available. The installation of courtyard features within the maze – repeatedly glimpsed, long before they are reached – and the use of revolving mirrors and projections onto clear-glass panels, triggered by movement within the maze, are new tricks now employed to heighten the mystery of the experience. The difficulty of finding your way through the maze is not dictated by a complicated layout, full of dead-end and false turns, but by the illusions and deceptions provided by the mirrors.

The perception that mirror mazes are complex and extensive, when in fact most occupy areas that would allow room for only the most basic of puzzle mazes, has made them an attractive proposition for the potential owner looking to provide a new attraction for visitors. A well-designed maze can typically appear to be six times its actual size. The mirror maze at Longleat House in Wiltshire, southwest England, housed in an old coach-house, employs the wonderfully sculpted framework supporting the mirrors to provide the experience of

BELOW In contrast to the maze illustrated opposite, this "Castle in the Clouds" maize maze at Tulleys Farm, West Sussex, in southern England packs many more paths into the available area with a regular geometric pattern that can be appreciated from the wooden bridges that span parts of the design.

wandering through an endless forest to stumble across a ruined medieval chapel in which the visitor may glimpse the Holy Grail, but only if they discover how to make it appear. Others are themed to re-create the feel of ancient Egyptian temples or the original seaside pier environment in which these mazes first flourished a century ago. A recent addition to the genre in Chicago uses the medium to good effect to simulate the subways and skyscrapers of the cityscape outside. The use of mirrors to deceive and confuse may be one of the oldest tricks in the book, used by stage magicians, cinematographers, and maze designers alike, but sometimes the old ideas, especially with a new twist, are often the best.

WATER MAZES

The idea of mazes formed with "walls" of water has been around for over four hundred years. Although long since destroyed, a maze formed of stone pathways winding between water-filled, lead-lined troughs was built in a courtyard of the royal palace at Greenwich, outer London, during the 17th century. Small water mazes, actually based on simple labyrinth

ABOVE *The mirror maze at Lucerne, in Switzerland, was originally constructed in Geneva in 1896 and installed at Lucerne in 1899. Extensively renovated in 1991, it is possibly the only surviving mirror maze from the late 19th- and early 20th-century heyday of mirror mazes.*

patterns were formerly popular decorative features in Islamic palaces in North Africa and the Middle East in the 17th and 18th centuries. These mazes were sometimes in the forms of water-filled rills or surrounding small fountains with the water falling and disappearing through labyrinthine channels, but, unfortunately, few examples have survived.

Although several small sculptural labyrinths with water running through their paths were installed in public settings in England, Denmark, and Germany during the 1970s and early 1980s, the modern revival of water mazes can really be traced to the innovative "Beatles' Maze," constructed by Minotaur Designs at the 1984 Liverpool Garden Festival to celebrate the rich heritage of the Beatles' music and as a memorial to the late John Lennon. A brick pathway winding back and forth around a pool in the shape of an apple, linked by stepping stones shaped as musical notes, provided access to a yellow submarine. The maze won a number of design awards but was dismantled when the festival closed. A similar water maze opened in 1997 at Hever Castle, in Kent, southeast England (to compliment the traditional hedge maze planted in 1904), features a simple pathway winding between densely planted channels that lead to a central stone tower overlooking the maze. Jets of water providing additional barriers to define the correct path prove an irresistible challenge to children on

BELOW *Confusing multiple-reflected images seen in a mirror maze were employed to dramatic effect in a famous scene from the 1946 film* Lady from Shanghai, *directed by Orson Welles, and starring Welles and Rita Hayworth.*

LEFT *The mirror maze at Wookey Hole Caves, Somerset, southwest England, shows the perception of endless corridors and immense space contained within a mirror maze. Typically, these mazes are only a fraction of the size they appear to be.*

warm summer days – lines of T-shirts drying in the sun often adorn the perimeter fence. Such water mazes are, however, at best, little else than elaborate water features; their ability to offer anything more than the simplest of puzzles is limited by their physical size and the considerable cost of installation and maintenance.

A new take on this old principle – and pointing to a different direction for this type of maze – is water maze installed in 1997 in St Hellier, Jersey, the Channel Islands. Occupying an open paved area, this example is formed of 208 water jets, controlled by computer with precision-valve technology, to create alternating walls of water that rise and fall to admit the walker to the next sector. It comes alive at nightfall with fibre-optic lighting. As the water from the jets immediately drains back into the grilles through which they emerge, it is safe for children.

THE JAPANESE MAZE CRAZE

The most extraordinary of the recent maze crazes must be the wooden panel mazes that swept across Japan in the 1980s. Originating in New Zealand, the first was designed and created at Wanaka in South Island in 1973 by Stuart Landsborough. An Englishman by birth, he grew up in close proximity to the hedge maze at Hampton Court Palace. Newly married

ABOVE *Opened in 1997, the water maze at Hever Castle, England, is set among aquatic plantings and provides only a simple puzzle, but the jets of water that block certain pathways prove irresistible to children. The central tower provides an overview and a quick (and dry) exit route.*

RIGHT *A yellow submarine, 15m (49ft) long, is the centrepiece of the "Beatles' Maze," constructed in 1984 at the Liverpool Garden Festival in northwest England. Although only a temporary installation, it was one of the first of the modern rediscoveries of the potential for water mazes.*

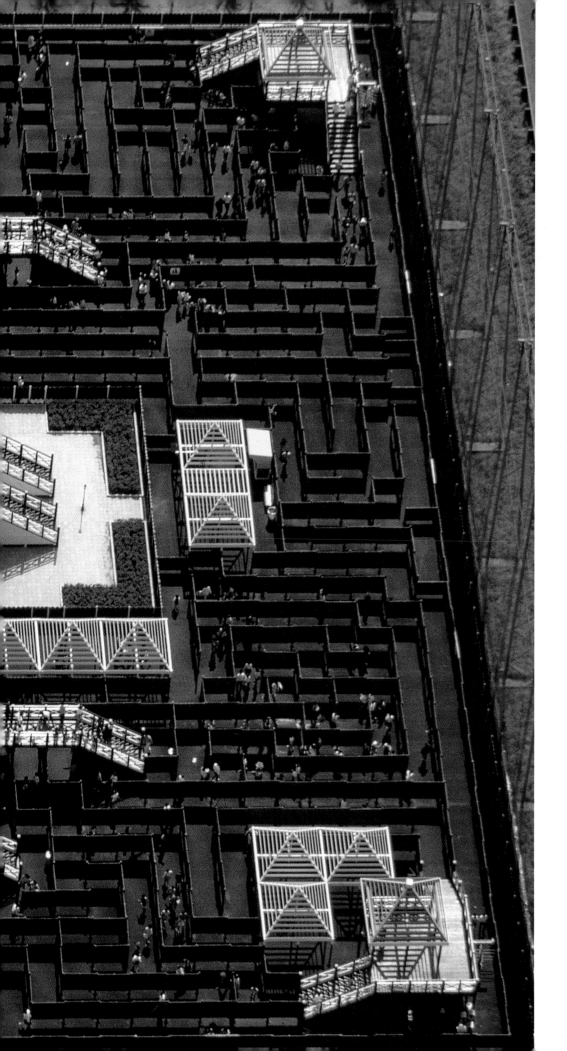

LEFT *A complex wooden panel maze at Funabashi, southeast of Tokyo, Japan – typical of the maze craze that swept Japan in the mid 1980s. Many of these mazes challenged visitors to solve the puzzle against the clock, with winning times posted on display boards. By the 1990s, many of these mazes had been replaced with new visitor attractions.*

and settled in New Zealand, he suggested a maze as a business proposition half in jest, but seeing the potential as a tourist attraction, set about designing a maze that would not take years to grow before being opened to the public. With timber in ready supply, his first maze had a kilometre (0.6 miles) of passageways contained within walls formed of 2m (6½ft) high wooden fence panels. It soon became clear to Landsborough that moving a few panels here and there could radically alter the complexity of his design. Three years of studying the behaviour of visitors to his maze provided insight into the psychology of the walkers – into their expectations and how long they were prepared to spend solving the puzzle before frustration set in. Initial results suggested that 20 minutes was long enough for most people.

In 1982, Landsborough added a whole new dimension to his puzzle: a series of wooden bridges that linked different sections of the maze. The addition of a third dimension to an essentially two-dimensional maze introduces further complexity without the need to dramatically increase the ground area occupied by the maze. The bridges provide enticing overhead views, and, if carefully placed, they are not necessarily helpful in solving the puzzle; if the base of the bridge is not found, however, the next section cannot be entered. The

ABOVE The 3-D wooden panel maze constructed by Ole Jensen in 1999 at Labyrinthia, Rodelund, in Jylland, Denmark. Based on the Danish national flag, it consists of four separate "islands," connected by bridges and overhead paths. The maze covers a total of 1,300sq m (2,550sq yd) and forms the centrepiece of a maze-related visitor attraction.

further addition of a series of successive goals, such as towers to climb in each corner of the maze, provide satisfaction along the way, reducing frustration and extending average visitor time in the attraction to 40 minutes. Increased sales at the tearooms and gift shop adjacent to the exit soon proved the value of this strategy.

By the early 1980s, a number of similar mazes based on Landsborough's pioneering concept had appeared in New Zealand and Australia, mostly poor imitations, but it was the export of his design skills to Japan in 1985 that triggered maze mania. Over four years he designed 20 panel mazes, each one bigger and more complex than the last, at locations throughout the country. Their success was phenomenal, and such large crowds were visiting the mazes that each new commission had to incorporate original ways of increasing capacity without diluting the essential object of the maze – to provide an entertaining puzzle. The later mazes could handle an incredible 1,500 people per hour without becoming congested. The challenge was to keep the crowds moving, and special "change points" were developed where a few panels could be moved to increase flow in advance of weekend and holiday crowds without seriously sacrificing complexity. Many innovative ideas were developed to entice visitors, such as souvenir punch cards to prove that the maze had been fully solved. Media interest in new openings and record times kept the interest at fever pitch.

The success of these mazes soon spawned imitations, and within five years nearly 200 mazes were built throughout Japan. Many were never designed for longevity, and sometimes they were just a means of generating revenue from a plot of land temporarily

BELOW *A variation on the theme of wooden panel mazes, the Celtic Maze at Legoland in Windsor, Buckinghamshire, southeast England, constructed by Adrian Fisher in 1996, is made of wattle fencing with a living willow tunnel included to provide an organic atmosphere. Based on the design of a two-thousand-year-old bronze shield found in the River Thames at Battersea, London, it is one of a cluster of three mazes at this popular family attraction.*

vacant between construction projects. By the early 1990s, the craze for mazes had faded, and the Japanese public had moved on to another entertainment fashion.

This interest in panel mazes as popular tourist attractions and obvious money-spinners meanwhile caught the attention of entrepreneurs in other countries and a number of similarly designed mazes have sprung up elsewhere. The "Wooz Maze" in Vacaville, California, US, built in 1988, featured night time games of laser tag. This maze has now been demolished and replaced by a new attraction. The "Maze of the Planets" in East Tawas, Michigan, US, is constructed in the shape of a giant ringed planet. Although the concept is only a little over 30 years old, these panel mazes will surely continue to prove popular and become traditional features of theme parks and similar tourist attractions.

OTHER MODERN MATERIALS AND NEW TWISTS

Modern plastics have also been used to create a number of novel mazes in the last decade or so. Portable mazes akin to inflatable "bouncy castles" are always popular with children. A large outdoor inflatable maze comprised of clip-together enclosed modules of multi-coloured vinyl toured parks and events across Europe in the mid-1990s and was a far more interesting development of the theme. The use of clip- or Velcro-together flooring materials to create infinitely variable and easily transportable mazes has been explored by a number of

BELOW Another constructional variation of a panel maze, this time using wooden poles set into the ground to form the walls of the maze, produces a more permanent and hardwearing structure. Built by Minotaur Designs in a children's playground at Bicton Park, Devon, southwest England, in 1986; the maze measures 48 x 22.5m (157 x 74ft).

ABOVE *An aerial view of the Bicton Park maze reveals the wonderful design by Randoll Coate in the shape of a giant foot. Moving through the maze, the visitor reaches each of the toes in turn. A roundabout occupies the heel of the foot.*

RIGHT *"Merlin's Magic Maze," a wooden panel maze painted in striking colours at Hollywell Bay Fun Park in Cornwall, southwest England. Entry to the maze, designed by Adrian Fisher in 1994, is through a waterfall that parts as the walker approaches. A series of smaller maze puzzles occupy the centre of this attraction.*

designers. Such mazes, laid out in minutes to a pre-printed plan, can be set up anywhere and have proved popular for children's playgrounds, educational displays, and as adjuncts to other maze-related events. Waterproof, washable, and slip-resistant, plastic floor mat mazes have been used on ice-rinks, cruise-ship decks, and muddy farmer's fields alike.

As with any two-dimensional maze, these plastic floor mat mazes provide only the simplest of puzzles when a traditional maze design is employed. While they provide ideal entertainment for small children, they have also been used to good effect to demonstrate a much more complex class of mazes. Sometimes known as "mazes-with-rules" or "conditional movement mazes," where you can move at any one point in the maze is conditional on your previous move or the instructions given at this point. While such mazes can look deceptively simple on the page or laid on the ground – just a grid of points or cells arranged in a simple square or some other pattern – getting to the finish is usually dependent on arriving at a particular adjacent cell in the correct direction. Dating back to the work of 18th-century mathematicians – Leonhard Euler's *Seven Bridges of Konigsberg* puzzle is frequently cited as a point of origin, and popularized in the late 19th century in puzzles produced by Sam Loyd and Lewis Carroll (of *Alice in Wonderland* fame) – these mazes introduced such concepts as "one-way streets" long before traffic congestion made them a reality in today's cities. Modern science and mathematics writers and newspaper columnists such as Martin Gardner, Steve Ryan, and Robert Abbott have further refined the principles, defined the mathematics, and developed many intriguing new variations on the theme.

Adrian Fisher, himself an avid designer and developer of "conditional movement mazes," has created many of these mazes in the form of plastic floor mat designs. The rules

BELOW *A "conditional movement maze", designed by Adrian Fisher, in the shape of a butterfly constructed from interlocking plastic floor tiles. Movement around the maze, always choosing a different colour path from the last, allows the correct sequence of "playing cards" to be selected to answer an environmental quiz that accompanies the maze.*

are based on number sequences, the moves of chess pieces, and designs where the correct movement sequence spells out particular words. Many of Fisher's mazes seriously challenge the common perception of the form a maze should take. While most of these "conditional movement mazes" may seem to be little more than particularly esoteric developments of the maze, designed for mathematicians and other "techies," the principles behind such mazes have a number of direct analogies with modern hi-tech computer chip circuitry design.

There is one group of people in society that would normally never be able to safely experience a modern puzzle maze, with all their clever visual effects and complex designs calculated to enhance the pleasure of visitors and catch the eye of those that provide publicity. For the blind, most of these mazes could prove a very troublesome proposition indeed. The construction of the world's first multi-sensory maze at the Royal National Institute for the Blind's New College School, in 1993, at Worcester in England, finally solved this problem. As part of a programme to provide a safe training environment for blind and partially sighted students, the maze simulates the dangerous and confusing world that everyday street fixtures and obstructions can pose for the blind. With different paving textures and fourteen different vertical hazards, such as walls, fences, and railings, and living hedges that provide minimal sound echoes (and are therefore difficult to detect), the resulting structure of the maze is a stimulating and educational challenge for the students.

THE RETURN
TO SYMBOLISM

The earliest labyrinths were nothing more than symbols, images applied in many ways, re-interpreted to fit the context of their times. It was only with the development of puzzle mazes that the path became more important than the pattern, a triumph of function over form, where visual effect was often a secondary consideration in the design. However, in recent years, the maze has been reunited with its emblematic roots, and there is a new generation of symbolic mazes and labyrinths.

THE RE-AWAKENING

The eye of the artist has always been quick to spot the pattern in the path of the maze and relate to the symbolism that accompanies those convoluted twists and turns. The popularity of the Greek myths among artists of the late 19th century resulted in numerous renditions of the scenes and characters from the original labyrinthine myth of Theseus and the Minotaur, a tradition that continued into the 20th century and is especially noticeable among the earlier paintings of Picasso, for instance. During the latter half of the 20th century, several artists turned their hands to creating actual mazes and labyrinths as landscape installations (*see pp.126–49*). While many of these are symbolic in the general sense, some have designs that are laden with carefully selected imagery and are worthy of study in their own right. Adding to this selection of artistic endeavours are the maze designers of today who appreciate the subtle ways of creating a maze with multiple layers of meaning, and know how to imbue it with more than just a clever pattern.

An important early example of the intentionally symbolic maze is the remarkable design for an installation constructed of high brick walls by English sculptor Michael Ayrton in Arkville, New York State, in 1969. Intended to simulate the Cretan labyrinth of legend, the design, set in the wooded landscape like a giant thumbprint, is inspired by the original classical labyrinth; however, it has a choice of pathways, as well as dead ends, which turns it into a simple maze. The high walls produce a claustrophobic effect and the long winding path leads to one or other of the two separate goals: one containing Ayrton's bronze sculpture of a fearsome Minotaur; the other a sculpture of Icarus taking flight, surrounded by polished metal panels. This famous story was a recurrent theme in Ayrton's work, and his etchings, sculptures, and writings on the subject are extensive. The construction of the Arkville Maze was in many ways the culmination of his labyrinth-related work, and a bronze maquette of the maze adorns his tombstone in Hadstock churchyard in Essex, England.

THE PATTERN IN THE PATHWAY

The revival of hedge mazes since the 1970s as popular features in formal and historical gardens has, for the most part, produced mazes that draw on traditional designs and forms. They are best suited to the aesthetics of the setting and create authentic recreations of the period. Many of the puzzle mazes built or grown for entertainment parks and similar locations are there purely to provide a challenge (consider the wooden panel mazes from Japan, for instance) and the overall design of the maze is often governed by the space allocated or the level of complexity required. The popularity of maize mazes in the 1990s has seen some interesting and innovative designs, but most are made for visual impact alone – eye-catching aerial images to capture media coverage and attract the visitors that fund the creation of these temporary giants of the maze world.

However, in the last twenty years or so a new aspect of design consideration has entered the arena, and today's maze designers often have an eye for the overall visual appeal of their products – essential if they are to stand out in the modern marketplace. The maze design becomes the logo – a pattern to adorn publicity material, T-shirts, and trinkets alike. This

Lurking in a recess of the Arkville Maze in New York State, a bronze statue of the terrifying Minotaur waits in his lair. The statue is concealed deep within the labyrinthine pattern created by the walls, to surprise the unwary visitor.

RIGHT *From above, the maze at Arkville reveals its nature. Designed in 1969 by Michael Ayrton, an English artist fascinated by the labyrinth story, his magnificent sculptures occupy the twin goals, each approached by a different route. This maze was in many ways the forerunner of the current trend for deeply symbolic mazes.*

new appreciation of the potential to introduce a symbolic element, whether in the form of a specific design component or as a whole, has revolutionized the field. This return to symbolism has become an integral element in the design of certain modern mazes, and, not surprisingly the original labyrinth designs – symbolic from the outset – have resurfaced.

Of course, the symbolism inherent in the design of any maze or labyrinth can be pitched at whatever level the client and potential visitors may require or comprehend. The designers of today's modern mazes have certainly recognized this fact, and, now freed from the need to originate maze designs that conform to the preconceived ideas of what an "ideal" maze should look like, they have produced some truly inspired designs. At their most basic level, these designs are simply fun; working in the family entertainment business, maze designers need to ensure that all those who see their work understand the symbolism and get the joke.

Notable examples include a brick-path maze set in turf at the Lappa Valley Railway in St. Newlyn in Cornwall, southwest England. Constructed by Adrian Fisher and Randoll Coate of Minotaur Designs in 1982, it is a representation, eight times the size of th original, of the Cornish inventor Richard Trevithick's 1804 Tramway Locomotive, the world's first railway locomotive. Walking the pathway, visitors turn to and fro on the cogs of the meshing drive wheels, and children can run the flywheel in imitation of the motion of its whirling speed. Hidden within the design are giant letters and Roman numerals that spell out names and dates for children's activity worksheets. A similar brick pathway maze, set in a courtyard at the Breamore Countryside Museum in Hampshire, southeast England, takes the form of four interlocking farmyard gates, with a topiary ewe at the centre. A simple hedge maze at the Kristallwelten (Crystal World) attraction in the town of Wattens, in the Austrian Tyrol, is in the shape of a giant hand. While it provides only the simplest of puzzles, its imagery in the context of a sculpture park is striking. A rather more complex yew hedge maze, opened in 1997 at the Parc Meli theme park in Belgium, takes the form of a giant seahorse, in keeping with the nautical theme of the rides and attractions. All of these mazes, and a number of similar examples, are firmly ensconced in the "family fun" category.

The complex, often symbolic, designs used for the increasingly popular maize mazes and some of the new breed of hedge maze designs from Fisher and others in the field have already been considered. Fisher's huge hedge maze at Drielandenpunt, in the Netherlands, is based on the heraldic beasts on the national flags of the three nations whose borders meet at the site location of the maze (*see pp.51–2*). Similar heraldic mazes have appeared at

RIGHT *Simple imagery is used in this brick path set in grass maze at Lappa Valley Railway in Cornwall, England. Celebrating the world's first steam locomotive, the maze is especially popular with children.*

several stately homes in Britain and in more public settings, in recent years, including a hedge maze at Blenheim Palace in Oxfordshire, central England, and one set in paving blocks in a pedestrian precinct in Worksop (see p.91). A variation on this theme, planted at Scone Palace, near Perth, Scotland, is a hedge maze in the shape of a heraldic five-pointed star, but planted in interlocking rows of green and copper beech hedges to give the effect of a traditional woven tartan pattern.

Slightly more complex than the heraldic mazes are a series of representational mazes designed around particular themes appropriate to their location. The octagonal beech hedge "Alice in Wonderland" maze at Hurn in Dorset, southwest England, is planted to a complex pattern that contains representations of the various characters from the classic children's tale, topiary figures for the suits of playing cards, and a raised walkway at the entrance to provide an overview that allows visitors to appreciate the design. A similarly symbolic hedge maze, in the grounds of the Château de Thoiry in Yvelines, near Paris, is based upon Francesco Colonna's 15th-century allegorical book *The Dream of Poliphilo*, which was influential in the design of later Renaissance gardens; the maze in Yvelines contains sections laid out to represent the various creatures in the story surrounding a giant eye with a five pointed star overlaid to stand for the five senses. These designs are aimed at an informed market, with a number of "in-jokes" intended for a knowledgeable visitor or for the amusement of the patron. Before considering these more overtly symbolic mazes in greater detail, a different category of installations must get a mention: symbolic labyrinths, often found in more private garden settings, and increasingly popular in recent years.

BELOW *Set in a private garden in Oxfordshire, England, this tranquil garden labyrinth, constructed by artist John Comino-Jones in 1988, symbolizes the artist's life as a journey, both physical and spiritual. The paved pathway set into the grass focuses the attention of the walker and enhances the detachment from the everyday world.*

As archetypal symbols, labyrinths have often been employed where a combination of an attractive decorative element together with deeper layers of symbolism designed for the owner or user is required. The recent popularity of the labyrinth symbol has seen a notable increase in these ancient devices built in private gardens for spiritual and meditational practices, sometimes just as a decorative feature, but intended as a reflection of the owners complex life or spiritual beliefs. Many of these labyrinths employ traditional designs and materials, often based on the turf-and-stone labyrinths in northwestern Europe or the cathedral labyrinths of medieval France. As many are in private gardens, it is not appropriate to give details, but they can be now found in America, Europe, and the Far East, with fine examples in Australia and New Zealand, and even in South Africa.

THE CHRISTIAN LABYRINTH IN SECULAR SETTING

The success of the medieval labyrinth design, developed in early Christian manuscripts and subsequently found in churches and cathedrals across Europe, was by no means accidental. The visual and mathematical symmetry of this design was key to its acceptance by medieval architects and clergy alike. This particular labyrinth style was the basis for many early garden labyrinths, which, as their hedges grew in height, developed into the hedge maze proper, complete with the branching paths and dead ends that defined the genre. Without question, the most influential example of this medieval labyrinth design is the version of it formed in the marble pavement in the nave of Chartres Cathedral in northern France. With its subtle embellishment on an already elegant symbolic design, this has become the labyrinth of choice for many of today's labyrinth builders. The dramatic revival of the labyrinth as a spiritual tool in recent years (*see pp.150–69*) has introduced this symbol to a whole new audience and provided it with a historical heritage and acceptability that has allowed it to transcend usage within a confined Christian context; this in turn has led to it becoming a symbol that is increasingly appearing in more public, secular settings. Yet this is nothing new. This same labyrinth style became widespread in the British Isles, for instance, some five hundred or more years ago, as the template for the turf labyrinths that sprung up on village greens and hilltops, as well as in the gardens of the nobility.

A number of fairly precise "replicas" of the Chartres labyrinth were constructed in the 1990s, especially in America, in public parks, and other open spaces. Although they range considerably in grandeur and permanence, in nearly all cases, the precise nature of the design and the historical connection with a medieval tradition is presented as an important reason for the installation. The simplest examples are created using hardwearing tennis-court paint and as outwardly decorative features in parks, children's playgrounds, and, more recently, in exercise trails and other recreational locations. Modern techniques of staining concrete with permanent colours have also been employed to produce some interesting examples and effects in these settings. One of the most impressive examples is the pavement labyrinth built in 1998 by Illinois-based creative paver Marty Kermeen, in Riverwalk Park in Naperville, Illinois. Measuring approximately 12m (39ft) in diameter, the labyrinth is surrounded by

ABOVE *Painted onto concrete in an exercise park in Greencastle, Indiana, by John Ridder, a labyrinth enthusiast from Indianapolis, this rendition of the labyrinth in Chartres Cathedral provides a striking meditative area at the centre of the park.*

amphitheatre-style seating in a splendid riverside setting, backed by mature pine trees. It has become a popular meeting place for children and families, and, early in the morning before too many people are around, for the ducks and geese from the river. The construction of this labyrinth took over 1,000 hours of labour, as many of the paving blocks required hand-cutting – the complex shapes of the lunations surrounding the labyrinth and the fleur-de-lys in the central goal, for example. All to produce a pavement labyrinth to rival the technical expertise of its medieval counterpart.

COATE'S CREATION

Returning now to symbolic mazes, the contribution made since the 1970s by Randoll Coate, one of the most influential of modern maze designers, cannot be overlooked. A retired British diplomat, most of Coate's maze designs have been for private clients, so they tend not to draw the publicity that other maze designer's more public installations attract. None the less, Coate's work is among the most innovative and by far the most symbolic of any maze designers. Long fascinated with creating mazes, Coate created his first installation, in a private garden in Gloucestershire, England in 1975; the design takes takes the form of a yew hedge maze, 57 x 28.5m (187 x 94ft), laid out in the shape of a giant footprint. Entitled "The Imprint of Man," the maze was intended to symbolize the owner's wish to leave an imprint

RIGHT *Marty Kermeen's exquisite paved labyrinth alongside the river in Naperville, Illinois, is another replica of the Chartres Cathedral labyrinth. It is surrounded by amphitheatre-style seating and provides a relaxing spot for parents to stop and chat, while their children play on the labyrinth, in an otherwise busy town centre.*

on the earth and the challenge of stepping into the unknown. The foremost toe, separate from the remainder of the maze, is situated on a small island in the adjacent stream and linked by a wooden bridge – incredibly, constructing the island and the bridge actually cost more than installing the rest of the maze! Entering at the heel, the path runs back and forth, visiting three small, enclosed gardens, before reaching the final destination: the big toe. The sinuous sweeps and loops of the yew hedges are far from random, and are composed of a number of separate design elements – symbols, numerals, signs of the zodiac, and the outlines of animals – one hundred and thirty-two symbols and images in all.

Coate's next maze, in the garden of the stately palace of Château de Beloeil, in Belgium, was planted to represent a pyramid; indeed the beech hedges have been trained to grow into an actual pyramid, 6m (20ft) high at the centre. The pattern of the pathway, viewed from above, traces out the name of the palace, Beloeil, although the actual route to be followed to the centre spells out the anagram "Belle Io". According to classical mythology the beautiful nymph Io, relentlessly pursued by Zeus, changed into a female equivalent of the Minotaur, half woman, half cow, to escape the god's advances and flee to Egypt. Such are the sophisticated games that Coate plays with his maze designs. His "Creation" hedge maze, designed for Baron Henric Falkenberg, and planted at the latter's home in Värmland Säby in Sweden, in 1979, is based on the Swedish botanist Carl von Linné's motto "Omne Vivum Ex Ovo" (all life comes from the egg); appropriately enough it takes the form of a giant egg. Dozens of symbols and figures can be picked out from the complex interweaving hedges, including figures from the Garden of Eden, a plan of the solar system, and the owner's initials. In keeping with the overall theme, the maze has two separate entrances, one for "Adams" and one for "Eves." Claimed at the time of its planting to be the first new hedge maze in Sweden for over two hundred years, it remains the largest and most beautiful example in a country that can already lay claim to the highest density of ancient labyrinths – over 350 stone labyrinths are recorded.

Coate's collaborations with other designers, including Adrian Fisher and Graham Burgess during the 1980s, have seen his design skills employed in the construction of a number of public maze installations, especially in Britain. The hedge mazes at Blenheim Palace, Leeds Castle, and Newquay Zoo, all show his influence and bear his signature, as do the "Alice in Wonderland" maze and the "Lion and Unicorn" street pavement mazes in Worksop town centre. More recently, Coate has been working on his own designs again, producing several private commissions, including a maze of fruit trees trained as espaliers for a private estate in Shropshire, and a huge hedge maze in the highlands of Scotland, inspired by the tower-like ziggurats of Sumerian culture, and planted and cut in such a way that four interlocking mazes imitate the stepped frontage of the temple at Ur when viewed from the goal.

The Marquis of Bath's remarkable collection of mazes at his ancestral home, Longleat House, in Wiltshire has been mentioned several times already – it is home to the hedge maze that Greg Bright designed in the 1970s, which in many ways kick-started the whole revival of the hedge maze as an acceptable art form for the late 20th century, as well as Fisher's lavishly decorated "King Arthur's Mirror" maze and Burgess's "Labyrinth of Love," planted

with old-fashioned climbing roses. The addition of a pair of hedge mazes designed by Coate to this maze mêlée in 1994, in order that they would be ready to open for the millennium, showcases the most dramatic and accessible examples of his work.

Acutely aware of the symbolism within the maze concept as well as their history, Coate has produced two installations, side by side. The first, the "Lunar Labyrinth", is, as the name suggests, a true labyrinth, formed in the shape of a crescent moon. Shockingly simple by Coate's normal standards, it is designed to correspond to the original and purest definition of a labyrinth, with just a single pathway, embellished only by a pebble mosaic at the goal.

The adjacent "Sun Maze," on the other hand, is a riot of exuberant design and complex symbolism, with a few subtle jokes thrown in for the benefit of its owner. All of the characters found in the legend of the Cretan labyrinth are represented, either figuratively, or by the symbols by which they are known. The whole story is contained within a maze that has the overall image of a glowering Minotaur's head surrounded by flames. While some of the imagery is only really apparent when viewed from a high vantage point (such as the private apartment of the Marquis, which overlooks the maze), the planting of both the "Lunar Labyrinth" and the "Sun Maze" with low box hedging, 10,000 plants in total, that will only reach waist height when fully grown, will ensure that visitors will still be able to appreciate the designs. Dressing the paths with 150 tons of peach-coloured gravel and the final installation of a mirror-and-mosaic-lined pond in the crown of the Minotaur completes what was one of the most dramatic maze installations of the closing decade of the 20th century.

SYMBOLIC AND EDUCATIONAL MAZES

While the complex imagery hidden within many of the recent maze installations has often been designed primarily for the amusement of their owners, a wider audience can also understand such symbolism. Children, as well as adults, appreciate the old maxim that a picture is worth a thousand words, and the multifaceted mixing of mazes and symbolism has been engaged to good effect in more than a few educational settings. The natural fascination of exploring the winding paths of the maze can also lead to an understanding of the message hidden within its walls.

Gernot Candolini, working mainly in his native Austria, has built a number of mazes as temporary installations at various events and festivals (*see* Working on a Smaller Scale, *pp.98–125,* for further examples of his work), but his "Dancing Jacob" maze design is of particular interest. Although superficially a maze with several short dead ends, the path is actually a labyrinth containing the image of a dancing figure, picked out by the "walls" of the labyrinth that run from the entrance into the centre. Candolini has installed this design at several festivals in paving blocks and flowers and has also produced portable versions, painted on canvas, to be shown at schools and events for the Innsbruck Catholic Youth Service. The labyrinth is presented once again as the traditional symbol of the trials of life, with the winding path the challenge for the faithful. The addition of the dancing figure represents the joy that is experienced when Christ arrives in one's life, and the halo surrounding the head of the dancer symbolizes the light of God's grace. By way of a contrast, the "Darwin Maze" at Edinburgh Zoo, in Scotland, with its choice of pathways for male and

female visitors and "Chamber of Natural Selection," where the walker's height and weight are assessed electronically to determine further progress, is enhanced with a decorative brick paving portraying a DNA spiral – arguably the pre-eminent icon of 20th-century biology.

Kentwell Hall in Suffolk, England – a moated Tudor house of some distinction – has for many years been the site of residential courses recreating the Tudor lifestyle, with participants, both children and adults, dressing in period costume to experience the everyday details (and drudgery) of 16th-century cookery, arts, and crafts. The main courtyard of the house was re-paved in 1985 with a striking Tudor Rose emblem, and the folds of the petals form a simple maze pattern that can be followed to the central chequerboard, large enough to play chess with giant pieces. The potential for mazes in such settings is unlimited, and a number of paving pattern mazes have appeared in school playgrounds in Britain in recent years (mostly the work of Fisher); however, the majority of these are concerned with numeric and literacy objectives rather than the straightforward symbolism of the above examples.

RELIGIOUS SYMBOLISM IN MAZES

To walk a maze or a labyrinth is to make a journey towards the goal, whether literally or metaphorically. Both the adoption of the labyrinth symbol by the medieval church and the pavement labyrinths of the Gothic cathedrals are testament to the appeal that this symbol held as a metaphor for the complexities of the journey through life on the pilgrimage road to heaven. Yet in many ways, life, as well as the road to salvation, is like a maze,

ABOVE *The "Darwin Maze," designed by Adrian Fisher, and opened in 1995, forms the focal point of the educational centre at Edinburgh Zoo in Scotland. The turtle emblem of the maze contains a number of evolutionary illustrations and activities for visiting school parties.*

RIGHT *The "Tudor Rose" maze, by Minotaur Designs, fills much of the central courtyard of Kentwell Hall in Suffolk, eastern England. Formed from 27,000 paving bricks, it adds a modern symbolic flourish still in keeping with the 16th-century house.*

and this point has not been overlooked. Three particular mazes, created in the second half of the 20th century, all owe their origins to religious symbolism revealed to their builders or inspirers in dreams and visions.

In 1950, the Reverend Harry Cheales had a dream in which he was instructed to build a maze in the rectory garden at Wyck Rissington in Gloucestershire, southwest England. The pattern appeared to him "as a pattern of white light ... traced ... like toothpaste from a tube." He spent five years planting his maze and decorated it with signs to remind visitors of the progression through childhood to old age and, finally, death. The choices and turns in the pathway represented the decisions and mistakes inevitably made in life; a tree already in the garden formed the central goal and symbolized heaven and eternity. Each year, on 10 August, the saint's Day of St Laurence, the patron saint of the village church, Cheales would lead a pilgrimage through the maze for parishioners and visitors. This continued until 1980, when Canon Cheales retired and the rectory was sold. Although the maze is now destroyed, a plan of it survives as a mosaic replica set into the wall of the church, dedicated as a memorial to Cheales in 1988. The hedge maze that was opened in 1968 in the garden of the Van Buuren Museum in Brussels, Belgium, has a cedar tree at its goal and a simple pathway that leads through a series of alcoves containing sculptures that illustrate the Jewish "Song of Songs." It, too, contains a wealth of religious symbolism.

In his enthronement address in 1980, the Archbishop of Canterbury, Robert Runcie, told how he had seen a maze in a dream, where the people near the centre could not find their way, while those in the outer circuits soon found the route to the heart of the maze. This sermon was to be the inspiration for the building of the "Archbishop's Maze" at Greys Court in Oxfordshire, central England, the following year. The design, adapted from medieval cathedral labyrinths, can be followed as either a labyrinth or a simple maze to an inscribed pillar with a sundial at the centre; the pillar stands on a Byzantine-style cross of stone, inset with a Roman cross in contrasting stone. The reconciliation of the various branches of the Christian Church was central to Runcie's life work, and the design of the maze, by its very nature and the marking of key points on the path, abounds with Christian symbolism. In many ways, it heralds the remarkable resurgence of the labyrinth as a tool for spiritual renewal and growth that would take off in the following decade.

LEFT *The "Archbishop's Maze" at Greys Court, Oxfordshire, England. Inspired by the enthronement address of Archbishop Runcie, the maze was constructed in 1981. The maze resembles Christ's crown of thorns and contains much Christian symbolism.*

WORKING ON A SMALLER SCALE

No longer is the labyrinth the sole domain of the wealthy landowner or the corporate investor with an eye cast toward visitor revenues. A little imagination makes the magical pathways of walkable mazes and labyrinths available to anyone who wants them. Combine that imagination with a little determination, the available technology, and traditional materials, and there are no limits to what people can create for their own pleasure. Mazes and labyrinths are available to all.

SCALING DOWN

High hedge walls and long confusing paths may be what most people think of when first considering mazes and labyrinths as garden elements, but these features are themselves merely creative developments of a once-simple design. With their broad walkways, towering walls, and high-maintenance designs, garden mazes came to belong solely to those with vast landholdings and substantial disposable incomes. Modern technology and interesting building materials have combined well with the creative license afforded by contemporary culture to provide a new genre that is imminently adaptable, affordable, and enjoyable.

The adaptation of traditional designs and materials to fit smaller areas, and personalization to reflect individual and local interests, has returned mazes and labyrinths to the "ordinary" person. For many, the creation is as important as the finished product, and, indeed, many have discovered that designing, funding, and constructing a labyrinth is an experience in community building, serving to draw people together. Whether it is a family working in a private garden, a congregation toiling elbow-to-elbow to create a sacred space, or an entire community providing entertainment and education for children, mazes and labyrinths are bridging diversity by giving form to imagination.

PREVIOUS PAGES *With candles lit to mark the walls between the pathways, friends gather at dusk to walk the turf labyrinth made by Jim Buchanan in his back garden at Caerlaverock in Scotland.*

LEFT *Set around a tree, this simple turf labyrinth is found in one of a sequence of themed gardens that re-create historic garden styles in the Dower House Garden at Morville Hall, Shropshire, western England.*

RIGHT *Turfed labyrinths are easily installed in any garden and require minimal maintenance. Even a simple spiral cut into the turf can form a fascinating garden feature, as shown here.*

LABYRINTHS FOR CHILDREN

Children are instinctively drawn to labyrinths and mazes. Wherever the labyrinth symbol is found, labyrinth games have always been invented and played by children. A century ago, in southern Africa, Zulu boys traced labyrinths in the sand, then challenged the younger boys to follow the paths to the centre that represented the chieftain's hut. So popular was this game that it was also played by the adults, especially after smoking hemp. In sacred settings, too, children succumbed to the lure of the labyrinth. Historical records show that in 1778, the medieval pavement labyrinth in Reims Cathedral, in northeast France, was dug up and destroyed by order of Canon Jacquemart, who complained that the disturbance caused by children playing on the labyrinth was disrupting religious services.

Throughout the world, new labyrinths and mazes are being designed and created with children specifically in mind. While any maze or labyrinth, in any location, is likely to catch the attention of a child, it can be easy and fun to place one in a setting designed specifically for children's entertainment. The simplest labyrinths and mazes attract children and spark their imaginative play, and regular geometric designs can easily be set into any tiled or block-paved area, or simply painted onto an existing pavement. Unlike adults, children require no introduction to the labyrinth and do not need detailed instructions for navigating the path. Left to their own devices, most children will naturally gravitate to the labyrinthine pattern and set out along the path to the centre, assigning symbolism and meaning to both the path

ABOVE *Based on the designs of the medieval labyrinths cut in turf, or laid in the floor of churches and cathedrals, this colourful labyrinth painted onto paving blocks in an Austrian garden provides a multi-purpose playground and racetrack for children.*

and its goal as they go along, and perhaps devising objectives and rules never dreamt of by the adult designers. It is often the children who issue invitations to adults to join them on the path and in the game.

Some designers have taken advantage of this innate curiosity and installed inventive mazes that require skill, knowledge, and logic to move along the paths. Schools have found these to be particularly effective ways of bridging the lessons in the classroom to the games of the playground. Modern peer-counselling programs for older children, particularly in the United States, teach interpersonal skills intended to intercept potentially problematic behaviour. For these programs, the labyrinth is an ideal teaching tool for young people exploring their needs for emotional containment and anger management. Walking labyrinths, it has been found, gives students the time and the space needed to think through problems and regain composure before acting upon deliberations.

BELOW *This is the plan and detail of a simple puzzle maze painted in a children's playground, with a pathway formed of cells arranged in a geometric pattern. Such designs allow imaginative play to develop, using the numbers and colours of the pattern as essential elements of the game.*

SIMPLE SOLUTIONS FOR SMALLER GARDENS

Installing a maze or a labyrinth in a small garden setting has become popular in recent years – a trend that appeals to adults and children alike. Many people, no longer confined by the traditional views of what a maze should be, are keen to explore the boundaries of what is possible within the parameters. Even a hedge maze can fit into a small space, but the whole affair needs to be scaled down accordingly, with low hedges and simpler designs. An award-winning installation by the Garden History Society at the Chelsea Flower Show in London in

2000 featured a simple spiralling maze planted in low hedging, based on a celebrated old design by the 18th-century French landscape architect André Le Nôtre. Flanked by a raised walkway, with wildflower gardens and water features beyond the maze, the garden is an amalgam of formal minimalism and baroque exuberance, celebrating the timeless quality of Le Nôtre's style, which can be seen at the palace of Versailles in France. The notion of re-creating part of a famous historical garden has obvious appeal to those with sufficient dedication. This garden at the Chelsea Flower Show provided a wonderful example of how those dreams can be turned into reality.

Of course, it is always possible to create a simple maze or a labyrinth using materials other than hedges. A labyrinthine pathway leading through raised beds of flowers provides a colourful diversion in the garden and an excuse to dally on the path and admire the plantings. A labyrinth of herbs, especially the flowering varieties, is an old design concept first proposed by garden writers in the 16th century. Often invested with much symbolic significance, such labyrinths were certainly built, although none survive from this period. In recent times, several modern interpretations of this concept have been built in the forms of both mazes and labyrinths. To wander between the banks of fragrant herbs, dotted with flowers and alive with insects, is a delight for the senses. Similar projects can be attempted with bedding plants.

The care and maintenance of a permanent maze or labyrinth is always a major consideration. Even a traditional turf labyrinth requires regular scouring of the trenches to keep the invading grass and weeds at bay. A hedge maze, however, demands a long-term investment of time to keep the hedges trimmed and the pathways in good order, and it also takes that plot of ground out of service for any other purpose. Flat, two-dimensional mazes, and especially labyrinths, are ideally suited to situations where temporary installations are required. Several ingenious techniques have been put to use in recent years to overcome the problems of maintenance and wear, all of which can be used in a small garden.

LEFT *Suitable for the more adventurous gardener, this small-scale hedge maze, installed at the 2000 Chelsea Flower Show by the Garden History Society, re-creates a classical garden style that could be adapted for any garden.*

LEFT *A simple labyrinthine pathway winds between raised flowerbeds with rockwork edging in a California garden. This idea is suitable for even the smallest garden, and is especially effective on gently sloping ground.*

Drawing inspiration from the traditional turf labyrinths on village greens in England and Germany, several designers have created mazes and labyrinths in open grassy areas by setting bricks and paving blocks into the turf. As they are recessed slightly below ground level, it is possible to run a lawnmower over the pathways without incurring damage. Otherwise, maintenance is reduced to little more than an occasional clipping back, where the turf begins to encroach onto the pathway. Labyrinth patterns are ideal in these situations, but simple mazes can also be formed that still provide entertaining puzzles. A good example is provided by Adrian Fisher's brick-path maze at Parham Park, West Sussex, southeast England. A pathway is built into the lawn in an intertwined looping pattern with no straight lines. It is difficult to follow with the eye, and it is to be walked with only one rule in mind – no turning back. Every fork in the path is a left or right decision, and reaching the goal is dependent on arriving at the final junction while travelling in the correct direction. Simple, but wonderfully effective.

BELOW *A labyrinth garden planted with flowers, and fragrant herbs, such as rosemary and lavender, provides a striking centrepiece in the larger garden. It provides particular sensory delight on a warm summer afternoon, when it is also a magnet for brightly coloured butterflies and buzzing insects.*

BELOW *This labyrinth is formed with banks of annual flowers, planted in soil between wooden edging strips, and has a small birch tree planted at the junction of the walls. Created by Gernot Candolini for the 1996 Tiroler Gartenschau in Innsbruck, Austria, a labyrinth of this style could be adapted to suit most gardens.*

The sculptural qualities of deeply cut turf labyrinths have inspired a number of land artists in recent decades; sculpting soil and turf in your own garden to create a labyrinthine path bounded by undulating walls or surrounding a central mount is a viable option for anyone with a strong back and a good shovel.

Simpler still is the idea of mowing the pathway of a maze or labyrinth into an open lawn area, although this often requires a large lawn to be effective. Cutting the grass for the first time, to establish the pattern, calls for some spatial planning and layout skills, and a line of sand or chalk dust to guide the lawnmower may prove helpful. However, after the initial cut it is easy to maintain the path throughout the summer. This approach has been tried by several botanical gardens and is especially suitable for situations where part of the grassed area is allowed to grow long. A twisting pathway leading through a wildflower meadow allows the visitor to walk between the banks of tall grass and admire the flowers.

However, where children are a concern, a more hardwearing approach is necessary. One solution to this problem that will last for a summer season is to mark out the walls of a maze or labyrinth on the grass with lawn fertilizer. The first decent rain shower will soon be followed by lush new growth in the pattern marked out, and the grass will grow longer and darker to this plan for the rest of the season, no matter how frequently it is cut. Of course, the use of a traditional solution, such as lime-based marker paint as used for tennis courts or sports grounds, is always a possibility, but it can be messy to apply. Environmentally friendly water-soluble spray paints are now available, and while they are usually employed for marking out building and excavation outlines, these too can be employed to produce quick and easy layouts that will last until the first rainstorm, or the lawnmower, comes along.

The solutions above are ideally suited for the summer months, but if you want to walk your temporary garden labyrinth in the springtime, as was the practice at many of the ancient turf labyrinths in Europe, then why not plant a simple labyrinth pattern into a lawn area with spring-flowering bulbs? Crocuses are ideal for this and soon die back to leave an open lawn. Every spring the pattern will re-appear to herald the warmer days ahead. What better way to entice you and your family back out into the garden to celebrate the approach of summer?

LABYRINTHS FOR THE HOME GARDEN

Many people now enjoy labyrinths in their own gardens. Often smaller in scale than those historic examples found along seacoasts and in village greens, they offer the opportunity for personalization to reflect some combination of the builder, the owner, and the setting. American dowser, teacher, and prolific labyrinth builder, Marty Cain of New Hampshire has personally installed several hundred labyrinths over the years, many of which are in gardens

LEFT *A simple hedge maze of low-growing hedging plants, such as box or privet, can be fitted into the smaller garden, as shown in this example. However, this usually provides more of a classical decorative feature than a complex maze to entrap and vex visitors.*

ABOVE *The graceful,*
looping brick pathways of
Veronica's Maze, set into
the lawn at Parham Park, in
southeast England, provides an
entertaining two-dimensional
maze, yet requires minimal
maintenance. This technique
would be especially effective
in a small garden.

or on private land. Her labyrinths are positioned in accordance with what she dowses as the geomantically correct position. Respect for the earth and its wishes, as guided by her dowsing rods, is her guiding principle for designing and situating a labyrinth.

Building on her reputation as an environmental artist, Cain has been invited to build site-specific labyrinths throughout the United States, and particularly in New England and elsewhere in the northeast. In her ongoing quest to learn more about the earth energies associated with labyrinths, she carefully studies and records her experiences with each labyrinth, and pays close attention to the stories people tell of walking on the labyrinths she has built. As a result, she now states emphatically, "I believe the labyrinth is an effective tool for many of life's transitions."

The home garden labyrinth, which can utilize materials ranging from what ever is simple and easily to hand to elegant imports requiring professional installation, often reflects the personal and spiritual philosophies of the person for whom it was built. Local stone, relics with personal significance to stand in the centre, and carefully chosen flowers and herbs can all play an integral role in the project, as can the shape of the winding paths themselves.

One of the foremost determinations to be made about such an installation is the degree of permanence it will have. Many home labyrinths are seasonal, designed to take advantage of the elements. Labyrinths mown into the lawns are popular in some areas where long days and warm summer evenings invite people to walk the turning paths until fall leaves and winter snows obliterate the patterns. In snowy climes, adventurous creators have been known to shovel the pathways of their designs onto snow-covered frozen lakes. Local ice skaters can even sharpen their techniques as they glide around the turns. Many of these frozen labyrinths then become the sites of candlelight walks and Winter Solstice celebrations.

For those wanting an even more temporary installation, for a child's party or an evening soiree, perhaps, basic designs can be laid out quickly using simple or themed materials to mark the paths. Forks or feathers stuck into the ground can be simple solutions for marking patterns temporarily, as can a trail of cornmeal – at least until the birds arrive to feast. A striking centrepiece for an evening garden party is a labyrinth whose paths are outlined with glowing luminaries or lanterns. These can be easily made by placing tiny candles on a bed of sand in glass jars or small paper bags. Indeed, an event held recently at an historic hedge maze in southern England featured a walk at nightfall through the maze, with the pathway glowing in the light of some 500 or more of these tea-lights set out in waxed paper cups. Clusters of lights at the dead ends of the maze drew the walkers like moths to the flame, sure that they were in sight of the goal, only to discover their folly. The organizers, aware of the unlit short cuts, were still able to reach the centre under the cover of darkness, ahead of the crowd of walkers, after first setting everyone on the path.

The labyrinth as a garden party element has historic precedence as well. The hedge maze installed at Versailles was the venue for many grand events at the royal court of the French kings in the 17th and 18th centuries. The owners of the "Jubilee Maze" at Symonds Yat West, Herefordshire, England, continue this tradition by floodlighting the stone pavilion at the goal of their fragrant cypress hedge maze on summer evenings to provide an additional pleasure for their guests. On a slightly less grand scale, maze researcher and pioneer W. H. Matthews records a garden fete that was held in Middlesex,

RIGHT *With low walls formed of bricks set into the ground, this simple labyrinth surrounds a small "stone circle" feature at the centre, providing a visual focus and counterpoint to the minimalism of the pathways.*

southern England, in 1921, to raise funds for a local church. At the entrance to the maze was a sign that read:

> Beware the dreadful Minotaur
> That dwells within the maze.
> The monster feeds on human gore
> And bones of those he slays
> Then softly through the labyrinth creep
> And rouse him not to strife
> Take one short peep, prepare to leap
> And run to save your life!

When the centre of this maze was achieved, the guests found a chair facing a decorated mirror in which was reflected their own image.

LABYRINTHS WITH A PURPOSE

Not all usable labyrinths are big enough to walk. While walking or running the pathways is always popular, some enthusiasts find great satisfaction and benefit in using small labyrinths that can be held on the lap or set on a table while the walkways are traced with the fingers or a small implement.

"Finger labyrinths," as they are called, are especially popular with those who consider regular labyrinth walking to be of benefit to body, mind, and spirit. Those who are fascinated by the mesmerizing, looping path of the labyrinth, but who, for whatever reason, find walking difficult, also appreciate them and believe that tracing the design with a finger gives a sense of the motion that simply looking at the designs cannot provide. Such considerations can even open up the concept and experience of the labyrinth to the blind.

Carved into wood or stone, these finger labyrinths are often works of art in their own right, affording aesthetic pleasure as well as providing a labyrinth for use as a meditative or spiritual tool. When not in use, these wood and stone labyrinths make striking wall ornaments or sculptural displays in homes or offices. Several manufacturers in the United States now produce finger labyrinths in a number of different finishes, but they are not beyond the means of the enthusiast with a basic wood-routing machine. Simpler paper, or embossed card, versions can fill the same purpose and are especially suited to travellers. Along these lines, a small sandbox with a labyrinth template inserted has been designed to give tactile resistance to the fingers as the pattern is traced. It is thought that this resistance aids the slowing of the mind so that a peaceful and meditative state can be achieved.

Spiritual counsellors and mental health workers who use labyrinths in their work can easily and inexpensively supply small paper labyrinths for clients and patients to take home with them for further use and practice. Therapist Neal Harris, based in Illinois, has designed a double labyrinth board, that allows the therapist and client to fingerwalk simultaneously. He reports increased trust and deepened intra-personal communication as a result of using these boards with clients.

BELOW *Formed of stone blocks set into a gravelled open space surrounded by plantings, this medieval-style labyrinth, in a private garden near Leeds in northern England, is essentially a decorative feature; however the labyrinth can still be walked as a contemplative exercise.*

Hospitals, too, are introducing both temporary and permanent labyrinth installations for their staff and patients. Considering the spiritual and emotional needs of both the patient, who is enduring a medical crisis, and those of the family and carers, the labyrinth walk becomes an opportunity for catharsis and healing. The symbolism inherent to the labyrinth often generates a personal imagery that can influence the course of the treatment, particularly in settings that already utilize art, visualization, and other alternative therapies. In cancer centres, in particular, the benefits of the powerful metaphors suggested by the labyrinth have been seen.

One use for the labyrinth today is as an emblem for peace, offering contemplative pathways, often with symbolic shaping and decoration, for walking side by side with others from the community. These peace labyrinths may be permanent structures incorporated into public spaces, or they may be more temporary installations and displays for intense short-term focus. The aim is for this symbol, with its complex and culturally diverse history, to invite visitors to reflect on the experience of traversing life's convoluted pathways, not with isolated aimlessness, but with purpose in community. For many, this is a container in which to apply the practices of their personal faith, whether it is prayerful walking, visualization of world peace, or simply onward reflection on the direction of their personal path through life.

ABOVE *A large labyrinth formed of boulders set in the grounds of the Provena Wellness Center, in the gardens of a hospital in Elgin, Illinois, where patients and staff alike can enjoy its circling paths.*

International peace groups are sponsoring the introduction of portable labyrinths to war-torn areas as part of the process for healing the wounds of war and addressing the resolution of deep-seated and long-lived conflicts. Trained teachers invite specialized groups to special events in which they offer the opportunity to walk the labyrinth and provide time, space, and direction for focused introspection, in the hope that workshop participants will take their experiences out into their wider communities. Often, the teachers are affected as deeply as those to whom they have introduced the labyrinth as a tool for peace.

Labyrinths dedicated to peace are appearing worldwide as a response to the strife and terror rampant in the world. Both large and small, many have been built in the United States as a way of commemorating the victims of local tragedies or atrocities. The events of September 11, 2001, which sparked the global war on terrorism, have given rise to a grass-roots call for peace using local talent, material, and effort. Many of these projects have included permanent or temporary labyrinths. Designed both to memorialize those who lost their lives in the attacks and to provide a refuge for anyone seeking to heal their own spiritual and emotional wounds, these labyrinths are largely the result of church or community efforts, although a number have appeared in private gardens.

Although many of these projects are small community installations, some are large-scale undertakings involving hundreds, even thousands, of participants. The recent opening of a yew hedge maze, billed as the world's largest, in Castlewellan Forest in Northern Ireland has been planted to commemorate the signing of the Good Friday Agreement in April 1998. The "Peacemaze" is the brainchild of anthropologist and landscape architect Beverley Lear, who staged a design competition for school children in order to encourage the idea of common ownership. Ideas selected from the 4,000 entries were incorporated into the design and construction of the maze, which is divided into two halves to represent the need to cross a

RIGHT *A large stone labyrinth in the grounds of the Mercy Center in northern Illinois likewise provides a place for reflection and contemplation.*

RIGHT *This boulder labyrinth, constructed by Danish labyrinth enthusiast Ole Jensen, is in perfect classical form to accompany his wooden panel maze at the Labyrinthia puzzle park in Jutland, Denmark.*

national divide, and shaped to resemble the human brain as a reminder of the thought processes required in the search for peace. Included in the maze are symbolic elements such as stepping stones to "teach us to take one step at a time," and a rickety bridge to "show the need to cross over and see another person's view."

KEEPING IT SIMPLE

Without doubt one of the easiest ways to construct a labyrinth of your own, albeit of a very temporary nature, is to scratch the design with a stick into the wet sand on a beach. This simple construction technique will allow you to develop your labyrinth-creation skills and play with the alternative forms that can be created from the most basic of the labyrinth designs. The classical labyrinth symbol starts with a cross, four angles, and four dots is the universal method that has been used throughout the history of the labyrinth, wherever it is found. Indeed, forming a labyrinth in this way may take you back to the ancient Bronze Age shores of the Mediterranean, when early sea-borne traders, with their ships pulled up on the shoreline and their wares spread out on the sand, would surely have shared with fellow traders the secret of drawing the labyrinth by just this method. How else would this most ancient of symbols have spread so far and wide in early, largely pre-literate societies, if not as a trick of drawing skill, passed from one person to another at the trading posts of this far-distant time? In just the same way that children throughout recorded history, and even to this day, share drawing tricks and paper-folding techniques to create games that will puzzle their classmates, or water-bombs and paper darts to infuriate their teachers, so the labyrinth has been a plaything, an object of amusement, as well as amazement, wherever it is found. Forming labyrinths and mazes in the sand on a seaside outing will always amuse the children as well as the child within.

On rockier shorelines, mazes and labyrinths have been built from boulders and wave-rounded stones from the beach for hundreds of years. In the Scilly Islands archipelago, some

48km (30 miles) southwest off the westernmost tip of Cornwall, in southwest England, there is a long-established tradition of creating these patterns from boulders. A lighthouse keeper created the oldest example, on the island of St. Agnes, in the 1720s, but in recent years many more have sprung up on various islands within the archipelago. This flourish appears to have started during World War II, when bored aircrew stationed on the island of St. Martins built several simple mazes of boulders on a headland on the island. This location is now home to more than a dozen such stone mazes and labyrinths that come and go as tourists plunder stones from old, overgrown examples to create new specimens by their side. These cleared sites then become the easel for the work of subsequent visitors and so the collection has grown over the period of sixty years or more to cover the entire foreshore. Winter storms occasionally lash the site, but also deliver fresh supplies of rocks for the next installation. Further stone labyrinths have appeared on other islands in recent decades. One example on St. Marys, originally formed in the 1960s, is now rather worn, and the pathway, deeply cut by the passage of numerous feet, is confused; others on islands favoured by day-trippers come and go almost year by year, but at any one time it is usually possible to find twenty or more examples scattered around the islands.

The Swedish island of Gotland, in the middle of the Baltic Sea, provides an even more complicated example of this tradition and the continuity of labyrinth construction by people from all walks of life over a considerable period of time. The earliest labyrinths on the island,

BELOW *A small boulder labyrinth installed in a private garden in Illinois. Tiny lights positioned around the labyrinth, with the addition of candles to pick out the pattern, transform it into a magical setting for summer evening garden parties.*

formed once again from boulders, are difficult to date accurately – they may be medieval, but some could be considerably older, even prehistoric. These large stone labyrinths are situated on headlands or other sites commanding wide views over the sea. The "Trojaborg," just outside of the capital town of Visby, is arguably the most famous labyrinth in Sweden; it is situated on a former shoreline (now a distance inland due to tectonic uplift of the coast in this region) below a rocky crag, where the town gibbet was once located. A similar example is to be found in a churchyard at Fröjel, a curious location that might suggest that the medieval church was built next to an already established sacred site from earlier Pagan times. Elsewhere on the island there are labyrinths painted during the 15th century as frescos on the walls of churches and also labyrinth graffiti, scratched by less reverent hands in dark corners of churches, presumably when nobody was looking. Several stone labyrinths situated in villages or next to schools are the product of 19th-century schoolmasters, who created these labyrinths as educational exercises for their pupils. Even then, it was appreciated that labyrinths could serve a multitude of purposes – historical and mathematical education, as well as physical exercise – a realization that has come to the fore once again in more recent times. This curious mix of labyrinths from a multitude of different periods is completed with the recent addition of a number of labyrinths constructed by holidaymakers, largely for the entertainment of children, at popular seaside locations. Mostly built within the last thirty or

BELOW *A stone labyrinth in the dappled light of a woodland clearing plays host to a family who chance across it during a summer outing. The wonderment of children is easily fired by such unexpected encounters.*

RIGHT *Scratched with a stick into the wet sand on a beach, this classical labyrinth is one circuit from completion.*

BELOW *The construction of the classical labyrinth symbol. This technique has been employed around the world for thousands of years to form the design of the labyrinth. Once learnt it can be carried in the head to create a labyrinth whenever the opportunity arises.*

MAGICAL PATHS

LEFT *A labyrinth formed from hundreds of small candles placed in paper bags weighted down with sand, popularly known as* luminaria *or* farolitos *in America, forms the setting for a musical recital and labyrinth walk in a woodland clearing on the night of a full moon.*

forty years, those that prove popular have survived and indeed receive regular attention as well as visitors, which has ensured that they have joined the collection of forty or so labyrinths that are recorded on this one small island. This collection of labyrinths, devotional, educational, and recreational, provides one of the most fascinating examples of the enduring appeal of the labyrinth across a broad spectrum of cultural contexts and interests over a considerable period of time.

Not surprisingly, these stone labyrinths, as easy to build now with little more than a pile of rocks as they have been throughout their long history, are proving popular with modern labyrinth creators. Equally appealing for most gardeners is their low maintenance requirements, providing the stones are firmly bedded at the outset of the project. These stone labyrinths are appearing in both public settings and in private gardens across Europe and the Americas, and, indeed around the world.

TAKING IT TO THE SCHOOLHOUSE

The appreciation of mazes and labyrinths in educational settings has indeed become an important aspect of this current revival of interest in the subject. The work of the Dane Jørgen Thordrup is a good example. A retired schoolteacher and leading researcher of the history of labyrinths in his native Scandinavia, Thordrup has been responsible for building a number of replicas of historic stone labyrinths both on school playing fields and in children's playgrounds in parks and gardens. Introducing the children of the school to the labyrinth symbol and its widespread occurrence and forms in a historical context, he then teaches the method of their construction and the mathematical and geometric principles that underlie it. The process is completed with construction of the labyrinth, where the children are able to put their new-found knowledge and labyrinth-building skills to the test. The resulting labyrinths are surprisingly popular with the children and are seen very much as "their labyrinth," not just installations provided for their enlightenment or entertainment. They also provide important springboards for other projects, notably historical and especially arts-based.

Likewise, Adrian Fisher has taken mazes and labyrinths into schools in England with some considerable success. Fisher's take on the subject is often more mathematically based than Thordrup's, and some of his paving installations in schools feature his innovative conditional movement mazes, with colour-coded pathways that provide the key to the rules of movement within the maze. Although only two-dimensional, many of these apparently simple maze designs are in fact as complicated as any three-dimensional puzzle and are capable of containing very sophisticated mathematical concepts and movement modes.

Their own imaginations stirred, creative teachers around the world are bringing labyrinths into the school curriculum to enliven young minds and capture the interests of students by using them as a case for lessons in subjects as diverse as art, drama, psychology, history, maths, and geography. In addition to marking the labyrinth's relevance as a historical object, progressive teachers and administrators have found it a useful addition to the playground, not only as a course to be run, but also as a refuge for worn-out students who needs a few minutes alone to regroup their thoughts and renew themselves before returning

LEFT *Laid in the courtyard of an elementary school in Plano, Illinois, the "Growing a Better World Labyrinth" involved everyone in the school – each person painted a brick, then laid it in place to form the walls of the pattern.*

to the stresses of the school day. Creating such a labyrinth, or a simple maze, in the playground does not require expensive equipment or materials. A pot of paint, in the hands of the responsible and creative, can be used to fashion a pleasing maze or labyrinth in little more than a few hours. Modern aerosol paints can cut the construction time to minutes.

Schools that recognize the applicability of the labyrinth to the curriculum and the social structure of the school have been successful in organizing students to instigate community efforts that have encouraged the learning of the many skills required for planning and carrying out such project; this, in turn, has fostered a proprietary concern for and interest in the finished labyrinth. Likewise, youth centres, Sunday schools, and children's organizations have found that sponsoring the building of such labyrinthine structures has increased community spirit within the organization at the same time providing a bridge into the larger local community. Young people seem to respond naturally to the labyrinth symbol and quite happily turn their imaginations to ways of making the ancient symbol relevant to their own lives and situations. Teenagers in one northern California community, for example, built a labyrinth at their Community Youth Centre to deal with their feelings of loss after a tragic accident claimed the life of local youth. Once it was completed, they opened the brick and turf labyrinth to the public as a memorial garden for anyone dealing with grief.

Labyrinth builders, Marty and Debi Kermeen, and their family, brought the labyrinth to their Illinois community by sponsoring a brick labyrinth in their local elementary school. Prior to beginning construction, the children were taught about the labyrinth and given an overview of the design and its history. Each student then painted one of the bricks before placing it in the school's central courtyard. Called the "Growing a Better World Labyrinth," it offers students and staff an ongoing invitation and reminder to examine their personal role in making the world a better place.

Along with the educators who are finding places for labyrinths within the walls of their classrooms, counsellors and social workers and others in the mental health field are finding them similarly relevant. One school counsellor, watching as a group of ten-year-olds negotiated the winding paths of a portable labyrinth during a school assembly, later talked to the children about how it felt to be walking on a path next to someone else, only to turn a corner and find yourself walking in a different direction. The children, who had been struggling with the shifting relationships typical of pre-adolescence, were quick to draw parallels between this walk and the dynamics of their own friendships. "Just because your paths go in different directions for a while doesn't mean you'll never be friends again," they concluded, "you just might meet up in the centre later on." Weeks later, they were still talking about what they had learned in the labyrinth.

AN APPEAL FOR ALL

Mazes and labyrinths hold an appeal for all – for the seeker looking to address serious purpose with symbolic creativity, as well as for the playful soul who builds for the sheer delight of the making and walking. Labyrinths and mazes capture our modern imaginations as successfully as they did those of our ancient ancestors, wherever they might have lived.

Whether you plan to build a glorious symbolic maze in order to fill your back garden and house with your collection of exotic statuary, or you merely wish to produce a simple labyrinth as a decorative feature, or to provide a little fun and entertainment at a family gathering or event, there is always an option available and within reach. Mazes and labyrinths, as we have seen, can be formed from a multitude of materials and installed for temporary one-off use or as permanent features. The adaptability that has taken them around the world over a period of many millennia is as vibrant now as it has always been. The only limits are the bounds of your imagination.

If you, too, wish to add a maze or a labyrinth to your life, be it in your garden, your backyard, or at some lonely spot in the landscape where you walk regularly or just happen across while on an excursion or holiday, the simplest solutions are often the best. While employing the services of a design genius, a land artist, or professional creator of mazes and labyrinths is sometimes appropriate and necessary, there are always opportunities to do-it-yourself. Experiment with designs and materials – who knows, in this rapidly developing field, you could just come up with a design concept, not yet tried, that could become the next maze craze.

EARTHWORKS AND LAND ART

The sinuous twists and turns of many of the traditional labyrinth designs have made this most ancient of symbols, with its complex history, evocative mythology, and worldwide distribution, a favoured stimulus for some of the modern practitioners of land art. The simplicity and adaptability of the basic labyrinth design, contrasting with the complexity of its symbolism, appeals to both the spiritual and secular aesthetic of artist, patron, and public alike, whatever the setting.

LABYRINTHS IN THE LANDSCAPE

The recent popularity and acceptance of art installations in the landscape, formed for the most part of natural organic materials – wood, soil, and stone, for example – has seen the ancient labyrinth symbols flower once again in a fresh field. With a new audience and the opportunity for placement in public open spaces, the adaptability of the labyrinth has captured the imagination of artists, patrons, and the public alike.

Given the materials available, the traditional turf and stone labyrinths of northwestern Europe have provided essential inspiration for a number of these modern interpretations. Novel forms of labyrinths and simple mazes, marked out in wet sand and formed in three dimensions with mounds of earth from construction spoil, have featured in the last few decades. These designs are intended to be viewed from a distance, or from above. While some are grand artistic gestures designed to leave their mark on the landscape, others are small and minimalist, just the bare bones of a labyrinthine form.

While many of the earliest labyrinths are essentially two dimensional, the traditional hedge mazes and many of the modern puzzle mazes need the introduction of the third dimension to function. Yet these boundaries are easily blurred, and just as some of the more complex, mathematically inspired modern mazes have now reverted back to two dimensions with the third provided by rules and conditions, so some labyrinths can be three dimensional in a very real sense.

Several historic precedents are recorded from the formal gardens of Europe, including a surviving example from the early 18th century in the grounds of the Fredensborg Royal Palace, near Helsingør in Denmark. A small mound in a far corner of the garden is encircled by a pathway, edged with low box hedges, in the form of a simple labyrinth. The placement of such mounds, to provide a pleasing vista across the owner's property, was a long-established tradition; moulding a labyrinth around these features was a most interesting development, but one that some would say had been tried long ago.

Glastonbury Tor, arguably the largest labyrinth in the world, is situated in the shadow of the Mendip Hills, overlooking the Somerset Levels in southwest England. Towering above the surrounding low-lying fields, which are prone to flooding in the winter, and known as the high point of the fabled Isle of Avalon – home to Druids, King Arthur, and the supposed

PREVIOUS PAGES *Cut deeply into the underlying chalk, the looping pathways of the "Mizmaze" turf labyrinth that crowns the top of St. Catherine's Hill, overlooking the city of Winchester in southern England, have a sculptural quality that has inspired modern land artists.*

RIGHT *Rising over 150m (492ft) above the Somerset Levels, Glastonbury Tor is encircled by sinuous ridges that have been interpreted as the remains of a huge three-dimensional labyrinth. Although no proof has been found, this explanation has gained wide popularity.*

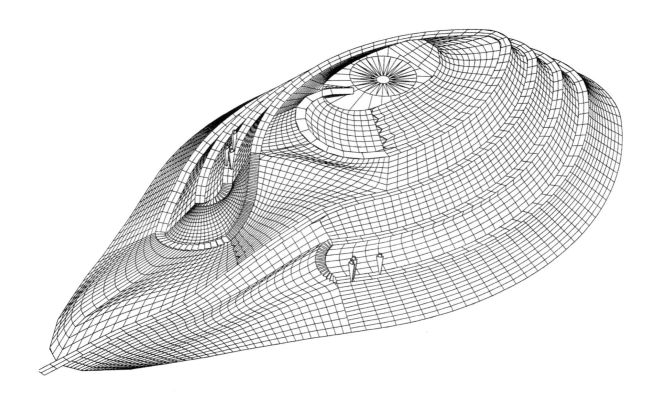

site of the first Christian church in Britain – the Tor is encircled by a series of ridges. Geologists argue that these are the result of differential erosion of the limestone core of the hill. Archaeologists, who have thoroughly excavated the ruins of the medieval chapel on the crown of the Tor, have never investigated the nature of the ridges and often explain them as agricultural terracing. During the 1960s Geoffrey Russell developed the notion that the ridges were in fact the remains of a vast three-dimensional labyrinth.

It was not until 1979, when Geoffrey Ashe, a Glastonbury resident and Arthurian authority, first defined the course that this supposed labyrinth took as it wound its way around the Tor, that anybody actually walked the labyrinth. Since that time, however, it has gained credence among a much wider audience, and thousands now walk the path each year. Despite the controversy that the supposed existence of the Tor labyrinth rouses, for no historical or archaeological proof has been produced since the theory was first proposed in 1968, the passage of those thousands of feet has worn a noticeable trackway, and the labyrinth most certainly "exists," in just the same way that a labyrinth mown on a lawn yesterday, or drawn in the sand today, exists.

Some have argued that a labyrinth on this scale must surely be contemporary with other great earthmoving exercises from prehistory, such as Silbury Hill in Wiltshire, southwest England, and the henge monuments of Neolithic Britain. While the Tor labyrinth can be dated back to the 1960s, the various claims for its historical antiquity may be, at best, contentious. However, its acceptance within the body of popular myth and folklore that surrounds Glastonbury has entered the Tor labyrinth into the collective psyche. As such, it is now the source of inspiration for other, similar, three-dimensional labyrinth constructions.

LEFT An isometric drawing of Peter Strauss's "Labyrinth-Berg II" installation at the Herrmannsdorfer Landwerkstätten, for the Hannover Expo 2000 event. The pathway winds four times around the hill before arriving at the summit.

BELOW The "Labyrinth-Berg II" shortly after completion in June 1999. A year later and the bare soil had been blanketed by grass, softening the outline, and transforming it into a striking, but apparently natural, feature in the landscape.

German artist Peter Strauss has long been fascinated by ancient symbols, including that of the labyrinth and he has produced several gallery-based labyrinth installations over the years. His landscape installations include a number modelled on prehistoric earthworks, stone circles, and burial chambers, but his "Labyrinth-Berg", constructed at Herrmannsdorf in 1994, was a project on a far larger scale. Covering a ground area of around 1,400sq m (1,674sq yd), and standing 9m (30ft) high, this huge mound of soil and stone is sculpted with a series of encircling terraces that form a basic labyrinth path leading to the summit. Although simpler in plan, the "Labyrinth-Berg" is essentially modelled on the Glastonbury Tor labyrinth, as was a similar installation that Strauss built for the Hannover Expo 2000 event. Entitled "Labyrinth-Berg II," this three dimensional labyrinth is slightly larger than the original installation – 50m (164ft) long, 35m (115ft) wide, and 10m (33ft) high – but has the same four-path classical labyrinth pattern.

A CALIFORNIAN EARTHMOVER

California-based Alex Champion is rapidly establishing his claim of being the most prolific contemporary labyrinthine land art installer. Although arriving late into the business after a career in research biochemistry, his output has been prodigious since he constructed his first labyrinth in 1987. Champion's interest in labyrinths was kindled after encountering them at conferences held by the American Society of Dowsers. Fellow dowsers Sig Lonegren, Richard

LEFT *Measuring 18m (59ft) in diameter, this labyrinth earthwork on a private hillside in Mendocino County, California, was dug by hand in 1987 by Alex Champion. This is his first permanent labyrinth installation, and the banks are planted with daffodil bulbs that bloom every spring.*

ABOVE *An aerial view of Champion's backyard in Mendocino County reveals several of his experimental labyrinthine earth sculptures. Champion's "Earth Mazes" challenge many of the preconceived ideas of what constitutes a maze or a labyrinth.*

Feather Anderson, and Nicolas Finck had been making labyrinths with chalk dust at the dowser's conferences since the mid-1980s, for experimental dowsing tests, and noted that people generally felt energized after walking or running the designs. Several experimenters had also reported positive health improvements, both short- and long-term, after repeated walking of the labyrinths. Fascinated by these apparent side-effects of encountering labyrinths, Champion decided to build one of his own.

The first was simply mown into long grass on his property in Mendocino County, California; however, following a visit to Ohio's "Serpent Mound," an ancient earthwork in the shape of a giant snake, Champion decided to make his labyrinth more permanent. Inspired by the sinuous shapes of the Serpent Mound and the embankments of the Neolithic henge monuments seen the previous summer during a visit to Britain, he set about creating a labyrinth in the same style, with a hollow pathway bordered by earth embankments. Whereas most people would start by finding the nearest earthmoving equipment hire shop, Champion decided to dig the labyrinth by hand, some thirty tons of back-breaking, hard clay soil, moved over a two-week period, to create a striking earth sculpture 18m (59ft) in diameter. The mounds of soil separating the paths were sown with wild flower seeds and grasses, and several hundred daffodil bulbs were set along the tops of the ridges. This first labyrinth, of the popular seven-path classical design, still survives, and is now cloaked in daffodil blooms each spring.

Bitten by the bug, Champion's next project was a small meandering closed-loop pathway, with a simple choice of left or right at the entrance, and set between rock walls in his front garden in Albany, California. Neighbours would ask about the "maze" in his garden, and Champion soon began to question the differences between mazes and labyrinths; after all, his garden maze had just one choice and no dead ends – effectively the same as a true labyrinth, where the only choice is whether to enter or not. A visit to the wooden panel maze at Wooz amusement park in Vacaville, California, clarified the nature of complex puzzle mazes, and a series of experimental designs soon followed.

BELOW *A clay and redwood bark chip earthwork installation by Alex Champion, for a private client. This swastika meander maze can be walked continuously with two choices – whether to enter and when to leave.*

Arguably still his most dramatic design, the curiously titled "Viking Age Horse Trappings Maze," based on a branching swastika design engraved on a piece of Viking metalwork found in Scandinavia, was commissioned in 1990 for a private property near Navarro in northern California. This earthwork has a complex swirling design that is redolent of motion and dynamic tension. Viewed from above, the plan reveals just one choice, a few turns inside the entrance, and a continuously looping pathway that dives inwards four times without ever reaching the deep rock-lined pit at the geometric centre, before returning to the start – is this a maze or a labyrinth? A double spiral earthwork, with the same initial choice of left or right and a path that returns to the start, fell into Champion's category of "Earth Maze," rather than labyrinth, and thus the working title for his constructions was born. In 1989 Champion left his day-job and became a full-time earth sculptor and builder of labyrinths.

A series of commercial commissions followed, with a fascinating selection of designs often based on isolated elements from the classical and medieval labyrinth types, with loops and turns adapted to provide a combination of visual effects and a flowing experience for the walker. All employ his signature style of sunken paths snaking between earthen mounds. Planting the mounds with colourful flowering plants, lining paths with coloured stone, and installing irrigation (essential during Californian summers) soon established Champion's reputation and a number of public commissions in his native California, and elsewhere in the US, have ensured a wide audience for his work. Many of his designs continue to challenge the popular conception of what differentiates a maze from a labyrinth, especially his minimalist designs, based on meanders, stars within circles, and interlaced knots and loops. Once the walker has chosen to enter the path, it can be walked repeatedly, looping continuously, until the entrance point is reached again, and a decision is made to exit. Champion defines these designs as "circular labyrinths," and presents them as tools for walking meditation.

With his initial introduction to labyrinths arising through his interest in dowsing – a field that nowadays involves far more than the traditional image of forked sticks and water divining – Champion has always had a particular curiosity for the more unusual aspects of labyrinth design: the energies, the patterns of movement, and numerical sequences of progression

through the patterns. Indeed, the interaction of his "Earth Mazes" with the numinous energies present at the site is often a key consideration in the exact location and orientation of his installations. His studies have convinced him that locating these symbols in the landscape can influence the flow of "telluric," or earth, energies, acting as amplifiers for these indefinable forces. It is this concentrating effect that, he theorizes, results in the reports of enhanced perception and positive health benefits from regular walkers of labyrinths.

Champion's project at the time of writing, in collaboration with other labyrinth builders and artists, is to create a line of permanent labyrinth installations in each of the American states cut by the line of the thirty-ninth latitude. Working with his wife, Joan, and Anne Walton, a fellow enthusiast from Canada, Champion recently constructed a labyrinth from large boulders on an army bombing range, to add Nevada to the list of states included in the project. An irrepressible character, Champion creates installations that leave their mark on the landscape.

ABOVE *The "Viking Age Horse Trappings Maze", dug by Alex Champion on a private property near Navarro, in northern California, in 1990. Measuring 21.5m (71ft) across, the complex meandering pathway is based on a branching swastika design, found engraved on an item of Viking metalwork discovered in Scandinavia.*

OTHER LABYRINTHINE WORKERS

Many internationally recognized artists have flirted with labyrinths during their careers; some make it a central theme of their work, for others it is simply a by-way to explore en route. The roll call of those who have included labyrinths within their land art installations is long and extensive, but it is worth taking a sample to illustrate the range of materials and forms they have employed. Richard Long built a stone labyrinth modelled on the Troy-town labyrinth in the Scilly Isles off southwest England, in Connemara, Ireland in 1971. Andy Goldsworthy, celebrated for his installations of stone and other natural objects harmoniously set into the landscape, designed the "Jolly Drovers Maze," a huge earth maze, built in 1989 on the site of a former colliery at Consett in northern England, and covering 0.8ha (2 acres). Richard Fleischner, working in America, has installed several labyrinthine works. His 1978 wire netting "Chain Link Maze," in the grounds of the University of Massachusetts, resembles the fencing around modern high-security prisons. The "Sod Maze" that he installed in 1974 at Château-sur-Mer in Newport, Rhode Island, is a turf labyrinth in all but name.

Alice Aycock's polygonal "Maze," executed in 1972 at New Kingston in Pennsylvania, was formed from high wooden stockade fencing. The claustrophobic passageways were designed to illustrate the more frightening aspects of choice, confinement, and isolation contained within the imagery of mazes. Michael Ayrton, although principally known as a sculptor and printmaker, created his enigmatic labyrinth of high brick walls on a private estate at Arkville in New York State in 1969 (see pp.79–81) to house several of his finest sculptures. Italo Lanfredini created a similar installation in a public open space high in the hills above Castel di Tusa, in Sicily, in 1990. Entitled "Arianna," this large labyrinth is made of cast terracotta-coloured concrete walls to blend into the landscape. A tall archway, reminiscent of the pierced monolithic stones guarding the entrance of ancient stone-built tombs in the area, spans the mouth of the labyrinth and symbolizes the entry into the world from the womb. At the end of the winding path, a small pool of water at the centre provides a literal chance to reflect on life. Joe Tilson has constructed a series of wooden labyrinths, and although not strictly falling within the category of land art, his work has been important in introducing the labyrinth symbol to many in the art world and creating an awareness of the form. The list of artists and their installations can be continued extensively, but it will suffice to look in a little more detail at the work of a handful of contemporary workers in the field to sense the range of styles and forms that are appearing on the scene.

A DANISH REVIVAL

Working mainly in his native Denmark, Jørgen Thordrup has created over a dozen permanent labyrinths and many temporary installations for educational and arts-related events. A retired school teacher, Thordrup has almost single-handedly spearheaded the labyrinth revival in Denmark, building his first piece, modelled on the ancient stone labyrinths from Sweden, and made out of boulders, in the village of Tulstrup in 1976, with the help of students from a local evening school where Thordup was teaching at the time. Restored and enlarged on several occasions, the Tulstrup labyrinth is still the location for the annual school reunion and is especially notable for the maypole dance held within it each May. With a tall pole, hung with red ribbons, erected at the centre and a flower-decked bower at the entrance, the image of people, young and old, walking the labyrinth with ribbons in hand is remarkable and has become something of a tradition within the village. The construction of a similar stone labyrinth in 1979 at the internationally renowned Lejre Historical and Archaeological Experiment Centre, a reconstructed Iron Age village where visitors can experience ancient crafts, technology, farming, and construction techniques, did much to popularize stone labyrinths; it has been especially valuable as an educational tool, drawing on their historical and mathematical aspects, not only in Denmark, but also further afield throughout Scandinavia.

Most of Thordrup's labyrinths have been constructed on school playing fields or in public parks, usually in connection with educational programs. As with so many types of maze or labyrinth, this association is nothing new. In late 19th-century Sweden, a number of

RIGHT *Surely the most ephemeral of all labyrinthine land art, Chris Parsons' remarkable work is formed by brushing patterns at dawn into the overnight dew on bowling greens in southern England. Within a few hours, the rising sun evaporates these unique art forms.*

LEFT *The stone labyrinth constructed in Valbypark, on the outskirts of Copenhagen, in April 1996, by Jørgen Thordrup with the assistance of local school children. This work is typical of Thordrup's installations at schools and playgrounds across Denmark; most are modelled on the ancient stone labyrinths found in Scandinavia.*

labyrinths were built by schoolmasters. Their locations near to the village schools often marks them out as different from the earlier labyrinths upon which they were modelled, and most of which are situated on offshore islands or remote headlands where fishing stations were established (see pp.28–9).

The involvement of children in the layout and construction of the current wave of stone labyrinths is key to their success. The children who worked on the labyrinth often take a personal interest in its care and upkeep – it is their labyrinth after all. As many of these labyrinths are located on private school property, they tend to receive only local recognition; however, the labyrinth that Thordrup built in 1995, adjacent to a children's playground next to the café in Valbypark, a public open space on the outskirts of Copenhagen, has become a popular gathering place for young families and their children.

While Thordrup does not necessarily view his labyrinths as art installations, his influence and co-operation with other artists throughout Scandinavia, who use the labyrinth symbol regularly in their work, has certainly made him an inspirational figure within this part of northern Europe. His involvement in the staging of a number of labyrinth-themed art exhibitions in the region usually sees him laying out another stone labyrinth within the confines of the gallery or museum, even though such labyrinths are normally only in existence for the duration of the event.

A ONE WOMAN EXHIBITION

The 2001 exhibition of land art labyrinths at Schlossverwaltung in Helbrunn, Austria, by home-grown artist Marianne Ewaldt, provided an excellent snapshot of one artist's fascination with the labyrinth symbol and the related forms that find their way into the labyrinthine field. Sculptures of Platonic solids, double spirals underwater, and triple spirals of boulders that encircled and linked trees together, were accompanied by labyrinths proper. A square classical labyrinth formed from mirrored tiles, lying at the bottom of a pond, was entitled "The Wedding of Sky and Earth." "Ariadne's Thread," a ball of rope unwinding to create the pathway of a classical labyrinth, laid on a cobbled floor, is rich with the symbolism of the original labyrinth story. Ariadne knew the secret of the labyrinth's path and provided the clew to Theseus – this thread symbolizes the course of life from birth to death, with all its twists and turns.

THE UNKNOWN ARTISTS

While many of the modern landscape labyrinths looked at so far are the work of named designers and artists – proud of their work and often documented in fine detail – there are a considerable number of such labyrinths that have been constructed with little or no fanfare, and often with no record of the builder. Examples are not difficult to find: some fifteen or more stone labyrinths and mazes on various islands among the Scilly Isles, off the southwest coast of England, were built with varying degrees of skilfulness by servicemen, tourists, and

BELOW *"Ariadne's Thread," a striking installation at Austrian artist Marianne Ewaldt's exhibition of land art labyrinths in the grounds and garden of the Schlossverwaltung in Hellbrunn during the summer of 2001.*

ABOVE *"The Wedding of Sky and Earth," a square classical labyrinth formed from mirrored tiles, installed on the gravel at the bottom of a shallow fish pond in the garden of the Schlossverwaltung in Hellbrunn in 2001 by Marianne Ewaldt.*

enthusiasts alike since the 1940s; another on the sacred island of Iona, off the west coast of Scotland, appeared during the spring of 2001. A series of stone labyrinths that have sprung up in recent years in Sibley Park on the outskirts of Oakland in California are the work of anonymous builders, although rumours abound.

Road protestors cut a beautiful turf labyrinth on Solsbury Hill, overlooking the city of Bath in southwestern England, when camped there during the late 1980s. Its windswept location, with panoramic views, brings regular visitors and dog walkers to the spot and the passage of those feet keep its pathways open – an accomplished artist would have struggled to find a better setting for such a landscape installation. The artists who constructed these labyrinths were inspired by the same combination of situation and symbolism.

ONE MAN'S OBSESSION

Working mostly in his native Scotland, Jim Buchanan has taken the symbol of the labyrinth as a core theme for his distinctive landart installations. Fascinated by spirals and maze designs since he was a child, Buchanan received his first commission to build a public labyrinth in 1996. Situated in Tapton Park, on the edge of Chesterfield, central England, the brief seemed simple enough: "what can you, as an artist, do creatively with 7,000 tons of sub-soil from an adjacent building project?" With a dumper truck and a sloping hillside as his canvas, he banked the soil into a series of concentric rings, 1.5m (5ft) high, linked up to form a huge classical labyrinth design with an overall diameter of 130m (427ft). Trees already growing

RIGHT *Formed with limestone beach pebbles, set into the grass on the shoreline at Nyhamn, on the Swedish island of Gotland, in the middle of the Baltic Sea, this simple stone labyrinth, built in the 1960s by an unknown holidaymaker, commands a panoramic view of the coastline. Such unintentional installations can soon become focal points in the landscape.*

on the hillside were incorporated into the design providing essential vertical interest to the installation. The scale of this project makes this without doubt one of the largest permanent labyrinths in the world.

The combination of sheer size and location hides the detail of the labyrinth from the viewer on the ground, and it is best appreciated as a hillside image from the opposite side of the valley. It can be seen clearly up to 3.2km (2 miles) away. Buchanan's objective was to create an ancient ceremonial *mandala* in a modern public setting, and a place where people, nature, and art could come together. The low fertility of the sub-soil employed in the embankments made it ideal for sowing with wild flower seeds, and each summer since the first year the labyrinth has been smothered in a mass of blooms swarming with bees and butterflies. The long winding path has proved popular with the local dog-walking community, and in the first winter snows the labyrinth teems with children on sledges.

Along with maintaining an earth labyrinth in his own back garden, Buchanan is always looking for new locations and challenges. Recent projects include mowing large labyrinthine patterns, based on the interlocking spirals of Celtic manuscripts and prehistoric rock art,

ABOVE *Winding through a boggy clearing alongside the Raider's Road in the Galloway Forest, southwest Scotland, Jim Buchanan's simple labyrinthine pathway, commissioned to mark the millennium, appears at first sight to be some kind of ancient excavated earthwork, hiding among the trees. A mound of stone stands at the goal.*

onto open spaces in western Scotland. Visible only from the air, they go one step further than the long-distance visibility of his "Earth and Wild Flower Labyrinth" at Tapton Park.

Buchanan always works with natural materials in challenging locations, and his "Millennium Labyrinth" is located in a boggy clearing alongside the Raider's Road, an old trackway that winds through the the Galloway Forest, near Clatteringshaws Loch in Galloway, southwest Scotland. A twisting path of crushed granite, banked up to provide a dry pathway, leads to a mound of stones at the centre, and forms a labyrinth of the simplest kind. With no signposts to mark its presence, the labyrinth is only just visible from the road, glimpsed through a line of pine trees. Situated in a landscape dotted with standing stones and Neolithic chambered tombs, the first impression is that this too is some prehistoric survival from the past, excavated and preserved, deep in the forest. The track leading down from the roadside draws the viewer in to explore and question the nature of this enigmatic structure.

While some of Buchanan's earth and stone-built labyrinths are permanent installations, his sand labyrinth, created on the foreshore of Irvine Harbour in southwest Scotland, had a lifespan determined by the time between two tides on a fine August day in 2000. As the morning tide receded, Buchanan marked out a simple labyrinth nearly 24m (80ft) in diameter. With the help of Boy Scouts and other members of the public, he dug deep trenches in the wet sand to mark the paths and heaped the spoil to form the walls of the labyrinth. By early evening the labyrinth was complete and a crowd had gathered to see this huge labyrinthine sandcastle face the rapidly advancing tide. Reaching the mouth of the labyrinth, the sea poured in to fill the sunken channel and raced through the winding alleyway, a group of children ran the path ahead of the water, as it was directed along the channel. For a few minutes, the equilibrium between dry land and the sea left the labyrinth's walls standing proud above the water, but as darkness fell, the labyrinth sank below the waves and the crowd dispersed. Although the following morning, the outline of the labyrinth was still visible as a series of undulations in the sand, within a few days all trace of it was erased, reclaimed by the sea from whose territory it had been formed.

At the time of writing, Buchanan is experimenting with labyrinths of light, projected onto the ground inside buildings as well as outside, after nightfall, onto the grass inside the ruins of abbeys and castles in his native Scotland. Equally ephemeral, a labyrinth of photons lasts as long as the power is turned on; the interplay of the walker's shadow with the lit pathway provides the dynamic in the equation.

IN CONCLUSION

Whatever medium and materials they employ, many of the land artists who have taken the labyrinth on board as a theme during the last few decades have turned to some of the oldest of its forms for inspiration. The simple classical labyrinth, as the forerunner of all later labyrinth designs, and the increasingly complex puzzle mazes, is infinitely adaptable and the natural starting point for further experiment. Many of the land art labyrinth installations of recent years utilize this design, or some direct adaptation of it.

Mazes, in the strict sense, are rarely the basis of creations by artists, for they are usually conceived to fall firmly within the realm of entertainment, rather than art. A labyrinth, even with a single path, may illustrate the principles of choice and confusion, and this ambiguity has always been part of their appeal for both designers and artists, adding to the sense of mystery for the visitor, many of whom, expecting a maze, discover a labyrinth instead.

Not surprisingly, perhaps, many of these artists are also fascinated by the mathematics, numerical ratios, and sequences inherent in the designs of these labyrinths. Couple these characteristics with the mythology and symbolism connected to the field, and it is not difficult to understand the status of the labyrinth as an art form, making it as popular today as at any time in its colourful and complex past.

BELOW *Soon to be destroyed by the tide that courses through its circuits, Jim Buchanan's sand labyrinth, dug into the beach at Irvine on the Clyde Estuary in southwest Scotland, was fated to a lifespan measured in hours.*

The preserved turf labyrinths of England and Germany, and the stone labyrinths of Scandinavia, continue to provide valuable inspiration for many of today's labyrinthine land artists. Visiting these ancient examples is, for many, akin to a spiritual and inspirational pilgrimage. The sculptural qualities of the turf labyrinths on St. Catherine's Hill, overlooking the city of Winchester, and the splendidly preserved example on the town common in the centre of Saffron Walden in Essex, both constructed during the 17th century, are often cited as influential by today's band of labyrinth builders. When they were constructed, they were not installed as items of art as such, but their gently swelling form and use of the living turf to create both a symbolic statement and an object for entertainment was certainly artful.

The rugged simplicity of the stone labyrinths in the harsher environment of northern Europe convey a sense of permanence, a natural pattern or fossilized form that has somehow weathered out of the ground. No surprise, then, that the themes and forms mentioned above are so clearly apparent in many of these modern labyrinth installations by today's new generation of land artists.

The use of these traditional forms in public settings appeals to clients and fascinates visitors alike. Whether the labyrinth or maze is modelled in soil or stone, the seemingly uncertain course of the pathway, which is safely contained within a defined space, entices the walker to follow the path, and see where it leads; it is usually the children that rush in first, free from the fear of the unfamiliar that develops through adult life. This accessible and interactive element of labyrinth installations tends to capture the imagination of all involved. The best examples have the added bonus of low, or even no, maintenance costs – something that is certainly a popular feature with the public authorities on whom responsibility for their future upkeep falls.

The renewed popularity of mazes and labyrinths during the last few decades, coupled with the current enthusiasm for publicly and privately funded art installations in public places – whether for the enhancement of the natural environment to attract visitors, or as part of land regeneration schemes in former industrial landscapes – means that there will undoubtedly be more of these land art labyrinths in the future, and their importance is destined to grow. The scale and permanence of a number of today's land art labyrinths pre-disposes them for long-term survival, to become the monuments of the future.

RIGHT *Surrounded by an embankment, the brick-lined pathway of the turf labyrinth at Saffron Walden, in eastern England, sweeps around and through the mounds at its four corners before eventually reaching the centre mound which was originally planted with a tree.*

THE SPIRITUAL REVIVAL

The winding path of the labyrinth has long been used for purposes that are significant to the soul and well-being of the spirit, whether employed to ensure the survival of childbirth, the safe return of fishermen, or the completion of a pilgrimage. Within the last decade, the labyrinth symbol has blossomed again, this time in a surprising context that has resulted in the construction of many hundreds of new labyrinths in churches and other multi-cultural spiritual settings.

AN ANCIENT HERITAGE

The closing decades of the 20th century have seen a remarkable revival of the fortune of puzzle mazes on a truly global scale. Alongside this revival, we have seen how the traditional labyrinths have also prospered. Since 1992 labyrinths have re-emerged into the light in a most spectacular fashion by returning to their roots. While we can only guess at the earliest use of labyrinths, there is reason to suppose that they were originally sacred dance patterns, used for some unknown ritual purposes. We know from the Roman chroniclers Suetonius and Virgil that Roman youths walked the labyrinth patterns, and indeed rode them on horseback, as a rite of passage and to celebrate the founding of towns and cities.

The use of the labyrinths in medieval cathedrals is shrouded in mystery, so little contemporary commentary survives; however, the walking of the pavement labyrinths by the clergy to celebrate the Easter ritual of death and resurrection is clearly documented. Tradition records that pilgrims visiting the cathedral labyrinths would walk the pathways before approaching the high altar to mark the completion of their journey. This use of the labyrinth in a religious setting was a continuation of the association of the labyrinth with spiritual practices – a link that stretches back for thousands of years, ever since the labyrinth's earliest appearance.

During the later medieval and renaissance periods, the labyrinth mutated into the puzzle maze and became a secular plaything – a place to dally or impress guests, and, in more recent times, to attract visitors to pit their wits against the ingenuity of the design. During the Age of Reason, the spiritual aspect of the labyrinth languished as a curiosity for antiquarian comment. The labyrinths constructed in European churches and cathedrals during the late 19th century were part of the Movement for architectural appreciation and education.

THE RESURGENCE

Yet the religious and spiritual heritage of the labyrinth has remained a potent theme. The first signs of a revival of interest in the labyrinth as a tool for spiritual illustration and guidance with relevance in the 20th century was probably Canon Harry Cheales' simple hedge maze at his rectory in Wyck Rissington, Gloucestershire, southwest England, during the 1950s

BELOW *With a background of trees hung with lights for the millennium celebrations, the terrazzo pavement labyrinth, built outside San Francisco's Grace Cathedral in 1995, has provided a public labyrinth in the heart of the city, available for walking around the clock.*

(*see p.97*). Seen by many at the time as one man's folly, it would surely have been embraced as a significant and meaningful statement of faith had it appeared a generation later.

A small labyrinth was installed in the crypt of Cologne Cathedral, in western Germany, in 1977, and several similar small decorative labyrinths created in churches and cathedrals also in Europe around this time are indicative of a new interest in the symbolism of the labyrinth. The installation of a copy of the 19th-century pavement labyrinth in Ely Cathedral, Cambridgeshire, eastern England, at the entrance of the then newly-built Anglican Cathedral at Pietermaritzburg, South Africa, in 1981, was likewise not intended for any particular spiritual purpose, but was a sign of things to come. In the late 1990s, several permanent labyrinths with spiritual intent were built in South Africa, surely the first batch of more to come.

There were also two labyrinths constructed in England during the early 1980s that should be considered in this spiritual context, although both are rather more symbolic in purpose and are not used for regular labyrinth walking in the way that the more recent examples in America are employed. The "Archbishop's Maze" at Greys Court, in Oxfordshire, central England, is actually a labyrinth, slightly adapted to produce a design walkable as a multicursal maze or unicursal labyrinth and, although spiritual in origin and design, it is essentially decorative in setting (*see p.97*). The pavement labyrinth set in the floor of Batheaston Church, near Bath, southwest England, in 1985 is a half-size replica of the medieval labyrinth formerly in the abbey of St. Bertin in St. Omer, northern France.

THE FULL FLOWERING

From this mere handful of examples placed in religious settings up to the late 1980s, it may come as a surprise to find that in the final decade of the 20th century, many hundreds of labyrinths were created in churches, retreat centres, and other similarly spiritually-oriented locations, especially in America. Within the last few years they have also begun to appear in Europe and further afield. Many of these labyrinths have been created to provide focal points for spiritual instruction and practice, sacred spaces for personal meditation and contemplation. Sometimes reserved for workshops and religious communities, many of the more permanent installations are open to spiritual seekers and casual visitors alike.

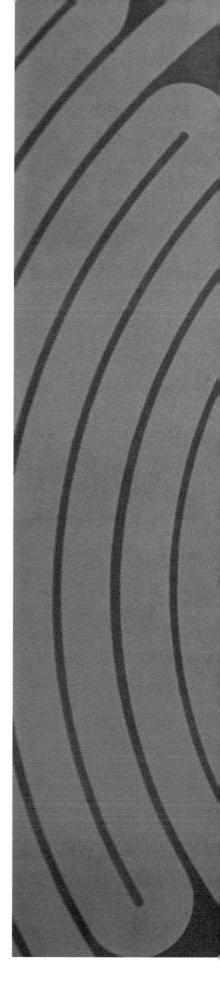

RIGHT *Many of the portable and permanent labyrinths installed in churches in America during the 1990s are modelled on the 13th-century labyrinth in Chartres Cathedral. Much of this popularity is a result of the influence of Veriditas and the teaching of the Reverend Dr. Lauren Artress (see pp.157–8).*

Without doubt the turning point in this current revival of the spiritual use of the labyrinth symbol occurred at Grace Cathedral in San Francisco, in December 1991, with the introduction of a temporary labyrinth – a replica of the famous example from Chartres Cathedral in France. Painted onto canvas, and laid in the nave of the cathedral for the 1992 New Year festivity led by the Reverend Dr. Lauren Artress, this example was used for the first labyrinth-walking event in a Christian church to gain widespread media coverage. Following a visit to the original labyrinth at Chartres, Artress and a group of volunteers pieced six heavy canvas panels together with Velcro and reproduced the ancient pattern in purple paint. During New Year's Eve, nearly 3,000 people gathered at the cathedral to pray for renewal, both for themselves and San Francisco – facing the problems of many large cities, such as AIDS, unemployment, and recession. Nearly 1,000 of those visitors walked the labyrinth, and the image of pilgrims on the pathway was splashed across the local news. Repeated requests for the labyrinth to be made available for subsequent events and specific labyrinth walks made it apparent that it had touched the hearts and imagination of both the parishioners and the wider public.

The fame of the labyrinth at Grace Cathedral soon began to extend beyond San Francisco, as word started to spread about the powerful experiences and positive benefits that walking it evoked. Before long, Artress was frequently travelling to churches throughout

America, with the canvas labyrinth packed into cases, to share her enthusiasm for it with other communities. A gifted and inspiring speaker, her book *Walking a Sacred Path: Rediscovering the Labyrinth as a Spiritual Tool*, soon become the standard text for the meditative and spiritual uses of the labyrinth and remains a major influence to this day. Her suggestions for considering the labyrinth as a three-fold walking meditation and ritual – walking the pathway inwards, reaching the centre, and then returning to the start point – has become widely accepted as the "correct" way to walk the labyrinth, although this is at variance to the procedure explained in Chartres Cathedral. Here, the pilgrim is encouraged to walk the pathway to the centre and then towards the high altar, with no return. Nevertheless, neither of these interpretations is based on any historical documentation, so either can be considered valid and appropriate. Whereas the symbolism of approaching the high altar directly from the centre applies only in a church or cathedral context, Artress's method provides symbolic significance for the walker in any setting and has become popular within diverse communities, whatever their denomination or spiritual background.

The subsequent founding of Veriditas – the World-Wide Labyrinth Project, a non-profit-making foundation based at Grace Cathedral, is committed to re-introducing the labyrinth in its many forms as a spiritual tool in cathedrals, churches, schools, retreat centres, hospitals, prisons, parks, hospices, airports, and community spaces around the world. Hundreds of people have attended the Veriditas-sponsored courses that train "labyrinth facilitators" to teach others how to use the labyrinth as a spiritual tool. Many of those who attend return to their churches or communities and purchase or fabricate a labyrinth of their own, which then inspires others. This organic growth process has resulted in a phenomenal expansion of the labyrinth network coast to coast within America and Canada, as well as overseas.

Veriditas, under the umbrella of the Episcopalian church, has also established a fascinating connection with the Catholic administration of Chartres Cathedral, and now leads annual pilgrimages to this cathedral to walk the labyrinth by candlelight. For many

BELOW LEFT *Laying out a canvas labyrinth. The ease with which these labyrinths can be set up, indoors or out, has made them popular choices for church and community gatherings, especially where diverse groups use the available space.*

BELOW *The design of the labyrinth in Chartres Cathedral. Precise replicas of this pattern, as well as a variety of derivative forms, have become the most widespread designs employed for the portable labyrinths that now travel the world.*

years, the labyrinth at Chartres has languished beneath the chairs in the nave, but of late, the cathedral authorities have begun to organize a regular timetable of days on which the labyrinth is uncovered for walking. Small crowds now gather on the specified days to walk its paths, an interesting parallel reflection of the sequence of events in San Francisco in the previous decade. A proliferation of books, postcards, and labyrinth trinkets are now available.

Eventually, the continual heavy use inflicted on the original canvas labyrinth in Grace Cathedral caused it to become worn and dirty, and in 1994 a woven carpet featuring the labyrinth design in purple was installed as a permanent replacement. This, too, remains popular and during the opening hours of the cathedral the labyrinth is rarely without somebody either walking its paths or contemplating the meaning of the design. In fact, this labyrinth has become something of a destination for labyrinth pilgrimage and in 1995 another permanent labyrinth – again, a replica of the one at Chartres – was installed in terrazzo paving in a courtyard in front of the cathedral, to make the labyrinth available to visitors for walking twenty-four hours a day.

MANY HANDS IN MANY LANDS

While the installation of the labyrinths at Grace Cathedral and the tireless work of Veriditas promoting the labyrinth in the Americas and further afield have both been instrumental in driving the spiritual labyrinth revival worldwide, there are other influences and individuals at work in Europe, America, and the Far East.

In America, enthusiasts in other regions of the country have initiated their own labyrinth outreach and educational projects, along similar lines to those of Veriditas. The influential work of Helen Curry in Connecticut, Robert Ferré in Missouri, John Ridder in Indiana, and Annette Reynolds in Alabama, among others equally dedicated to the cause, has brought the labyrinth to a wide audience in a number of imaginative ways. Ferré's construction of a large indoor labyrinth from canned food donated for a charity appeal for the homeless ensured wide and entertaining coverage, essential to introduce the labyrinth to a suspicious and media-jaded public. Many of these keen labyrinth envoys were involved in the founding of the Labyrinth Society in 1998 to provide an educational and support body for those working with labyrinths in all fields, not just the spiritually-based areas that are catered for by other organisations. The Society sponsored events and programs now taking place are destined to bring labyrinths to an even wider and more diverse audience.

Of course, labyrinths designed to be symbolic of spiritual quests have appeared in America on previous occasions. The hedge labyrinths planted by the Harmonists, a dissident religious sect from Germany that settled in Pennsylvania and Indiana in the early 1800s, were

ABOVE A labyrinth walk in progress at the Omega Centre in Rhinebeck, New York, during the 1996 annual labyrinth conference. Painted onto canvas with phosphorescent paint, the labyrinth glows with an eerie light under ultra-violet lighting.

employed to represent the group's search for spiritual perfection. The re-created hedge maze at New Harmony, Indiana, planted in 1941 and based upon the plan of the original c.1815 hedge labyrinth at New Harmony, has now been joined by a stunning modern replica of the Chartres Cathedral labyrinth. Commissioned by Jane Blaffer Owen, a descendant of the Owen family that purchased the town from the Harmonists in 1824, it is a precise full-scale copy, created using advanced computer-based techniques, and etched onto polished interlocking blocks of granite, set in a small park in the town. The layout of the park is based upon the sacred geometry of the nave of the cathedral, and, fittingly, the labyrinth was dedicated by Canon Legaux, Rector of Chartres Cathedral, in October 1997.

Illinois-based paving artist Marty Kermeen has created a number of pavement labyrinths within the precincts of churches across America since 1997. It is interesting to note that these churches cover a broad range of denominations from the traditional to the contemporary. Tailored to fit both the available space and budget, Kermeen's hand-built paver labyrinths reflect the loving and meticulous craftsmanship that has become his trademark. While these church labyrinths have value for their beauty alone, the function they fulfil in the community is beyond calculation. His "Knoxville" labyrinth in Tennessee, for example, was the scene of a remarkable and spontaneous gathering that occurred immediately after the terrorist attacks on September 11, 2001. On hearing the news, crowds of people from the downtown area began arriving at the labyrinth, and long lines formed, as people walked the spiralling paths in order to come to grips with their tumultuous emotions. Other labyrinth builders in America have also been busy. Notable among these is David Tolzman, of New York, whose stained-concrete techniques have provided quick and low-cost solutions for communities and church groups seeking labyrinths of their own.

The construction of a replica of the Chartres labyrinth in 1993 at the Trappist monastery of St. Remy in Rochefort, in the Ardennes, Belgium, is typical of the current interest in the labyrinth pattern in Europe. In the German-speaking countries of Europe there has been a similar flowering of labyrinths in a spiritual context, taking place since the late 1980s, presaged by the installation of a simple tile labyrinth in the church at Hohenberg in Ellwangen,

LEFT *Sewn from panels of fabric in a rainbow of hues, this portable labyrinth, based on the classical design, can be installed in a small room and packed away into a shoulder bag. This is a labyrinth for any location.*

southern Germany, in 1985. Several labyrinths have been installed within Lutheran churches and seminaries in Austria and Germany in recent years, and many of these are the work of women's groups. Along with a number of installations in public open spaces, the Zurich-based Labyrinth Project International group has created labyrinths in churches, both Catholic and Protestant, as well as in the grounds of retreat centres. Artist Agnes Barmettler, art lecturer Rosmarie Scmidt, and Susanne Kramer-Friedrich are among the most productive workers in the region, and have recently installed labyrinths in women's prisons to bring the contemplative as well as spiritual aspects of the labyrinth into the lives of long-term inmates. Prisoners are encouraged to tend the labyrinth formed of plants and stones situated in the exercise yard, and the reports of positive results from the prison staff parallel the stories coming from the "prison ministries" in America, where volunteers take canvas labyrinths into high-security prison facilities on an ongoing basis.

Within the last few years, this spiritual labyrinth revival has reached New Zealand and Australia with several beautiful outdoor labyrinths – of the Chartres pattern – installed in the grounds of religious retreats and similar spiritually inclined establishments. A splendid illustration of the dedication and community spirit that is fostered by the construction of these labyrinths is provided by the example completed in September 1999 at the Frederick Wallis House retreat at Lower Hutt, on the outskirts of Wellington, New Zealand. The intricate tile mosaic that forms the walls of the labyrinth took a thousand hours of work, over an eight-month period, to complete. In total, over sixty-five people – moslty volunteers – worked on the labyrinth at different stages of its construction. During the first few years of the 21st century, temporary labyrinths have begun to appear regularly in churches and cathedrals in England, and it can surely be only a matter of time before another permanent labyrinth is installed in Britain as a consequence of these introductions, if the pattern of events witnessed elsewhere is any indication.

PORTABLE LABYRINTHS

One of the most fascinating aspects of this new-found appeal of the labyrinth in a spiritual setting is the means by which it most commonly travels and makes its introduction to new groups of enthusiasts. The portable labyrinth, usually painted onto canvas or some other

RIGHT *Exemplifying another innovative approach, this labyrinth is formed from strips and pre-cut shapes of industrial carpet. Joined with Velcro, and attached to the floor with double-sided adhesive tape, the carpet strips provide an extra tactile element when walked barefoot in a candle-lit room.*

fabric, was popularized by Lauren Artress as she travelled with the canvas labyrinths produced at Grace Cathedral. To overcome the challenges of moving a large piece of canvas around they addressed this problem by fabricating the labyrinth as a number of separate overlapping strips, held together with Velcro. Packed into snap-top plastic packing boxes, these labyrinths may be loaded into the trunk of a vehicle or onto an aircraft with comparative ease.

However, a full sized "traditional" canvas labyrinth, between 9–12m (30–40ft) in diameter, still weighs in at around 45kg (100lb), and the need to take these labyrinths "on the road" has created some innovative solutions to the problem of improving their portability. Within the last few years, several of the portable labyrinth manufactures in America have produced labyrinths painted onto plastic-coated fabric, which is lighter, hardwearing, and easy to clean. They address many of the problems that accompany regular canvas, but need to be folded carefully to avoid permanent creases forming in the fabric. Ultra-lightweight nylon sailcloth labyrinths have also been produced, and while they can be prone to slipping on polished floors, they pack easily into small cases and can even be stowed in overhead luggage lockers onboard aircraft. The ultimate lightweight solution for certain presenters has been the use of specialist adhesive tapes, suitable on a multitude of floor surfaces, but these require a considerable degree of skill for quick and accurate layout.

The remarkable interest that the labyrinth has generated in the 1990s has seen these portable labyrinths travel back and forth across the Americas, to Europe, Southern Africa and the Far East, for presentations, religious retreats, and residential courses exploring the spiritual and meditative uses of the labyrinth. They are also a regular feature at arts and community events and have become surprisingly important in introducing this ancient symbol to a new generation. With many people already familiar with puzzle mazes as a result of the popularity of maize mazes in the early 1990s, and the increasing number of mazes installed at stately houses or in entertainment parks, labyrinths are no longer difficult to comprehend. As is so commonly the case with the puzzle mazes, it is often the curiosity and excitement of children that paves the way for adults to follow and explore the lure of the labyrinth.

Hundreds of portable labyrinths have been produced since the early 1990s, and while it is difficult to find reliable estimates, it is clear that many hundreds of thousands, maybe millions, of people around the world have encountered the labyrinth through this medium. However, it would be wrong to think that these portable labyrinths are being mass-produced. Each one is hand painted, and while many are created by individuals or community groups for use within their immediate circle, several labyrinth enthusiasts in America, most notably Robert Ferré in St. Louis and John Ridder in Indianapolis, have created a veritable cottage industry producing these labyrinths to order, in a range of styles and materials.

Replicas of the Chartres labyrinth remain popular, especially with more traditional church communities, although the space required for laying out a 9m (30ft) plus canvas has driven the development of a number of "cut-down" versions of the design, with fewer circuits to fit a smaller canvas, which still retain the essence of the original form. The archetypal classical labyrinth pattern also figures frequently. These are more commonly found in use outside the customary Christian religious settings, among "New Age" or pagan communities, although

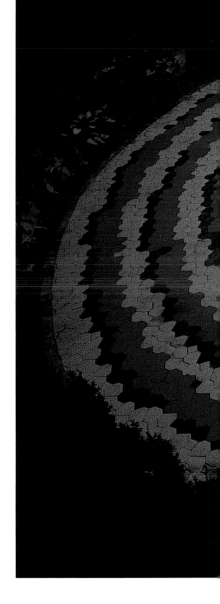

ABOVE *Installed in 2000, to a design created by Adrian Fisher, this paving labyrinth on a private estate in Connecticut, was created in memory of a resident's son. Set in a woodland clearing and surrounded by shrubs, the rugged pathway leads to a central "Tree of Life" mosaic.*

these groups are often exploring the same spiritual paths, but sometimes take a conscious decision to use a less-overtly Christian labyrinth. The seven concentric paths of the classical labyrinth have become associated with the seven colours of the rainbow and the seven chakras, the "energy centres" of the human body, in popular literature within the field. Quite a few of the portable classical labyrinths have their paths painted in spectrums of colours to both "channel the energies" and create striking visual effects.

With the advent and rapid expansion of the Internet, the promotion and marketing of these portable labyrinths, not to mention a plethora of labyrinth-related products and spiritual services, has boomed in recent years. On-line labyrinths are big business, and a number of websites now exist where a labyrinth design can be chosen and a portable labyrinth commissioned to fit individual requirements and budget. Not surprisingly, in this commercial environment, some labyrinth designers have sought to protect their design innovations with copyrighting. This has generated much discussion and raised some interesting points concerning the claims to exclusive use of designs and names for labyrinth styles that have been in use for many hundreds, or even thousands, of years. If the history of mazes and labyrinths illustrates one fact over all others, it is that the most meaningful and pleasing designs are

LEFT *Small lamps that
accumulate charges
throughout the day from solar
panels automatically illuminate
this stone labyrinth in the
grounds of the Buck Horn Inn,
near Gatlinburg, Tennessee, as
the light fades at dusk. This
labyrinth is a fitting memorial
to a daughter who died
tragically young.*

destined to be copied over and over again, for many generations to come. If the designers of the labyrinth in Chartres Cathedral only had a dollar for every copy of their creation…

RETREATS AND REMEMBRANCE

Not all of these recent spiritually-inspired labyrinths have been constructed within churches and their gardens. A considerable number are situated in the grounds of retreat centres and similar establishments designed to appeal to the spiritual seeker. Here, the labyrinths are often presented as reflective islands of tranquillity in a chaotic world. No longer the sole domain of religious and spiritual groups, these retreat settings are also increasingly being used for corporate team-building and stress-relief workshops. Several labyrinth teachers have reported considerable success introducing the labyrinth into this environment. The winding path of the labyrinth invites the walker to clear the mind, quieten the pace, and refresh the soul.

While much of this philosophy might seem to be rather esoteric, the recent appearance of several permanent labyrinths within the grounds of hospitals, medical schools, and hospices may appear at first sight to be a startling acceptance of a fringe concept in a traditionally and increasingly scientific field. However, as a doctor at one of these hospitals was heard to remark, "Medicine can cure the body, but this is a tool for curing the soul." Perhaps this gives credence to the claims of the benefits of labyrinth walking that have been circulating and rippling outwards in ever widening circles during the last decade.

By far the most touching of the recent labyrinth installations are those created as memorials to loved ones taken before their time. The tortuous twisting path of the labyrinth – a path that relentlessly leads to its conclusion, with no opportunity for turning back – has proved a powerful metaphor for people seeking to come to terms with the painful loss of friends or family members. The installation of a labyrinth as a memorial provides the opportunity to walk the path of life. The labyrinth becomes a contained space for a quiet contemplative exercise, a place to let down one's guard and fully experience the depth of one's feelings and emotions. It offers the chance to rekindle happy memories and creates an interface between this world and the beyond. This, too, draws on an ancient and long established tradition. The ancient stone labyrinths found in Sweden and Arctic Russia, situated alongside prehistoric grave fields, are considered by some scholars to have served just the same purpose.

THE SEARCH FOR REASON

This remarkable renaissance of the labyrinth within the last decade or so begs the biggest question of all: what is it about this most ancient of symbols that has suddenly spurred this new found interest and relevance within the lives and spiritual beliefs and practices of a whole generation in such a short period of time?

One of the reasons for the acceptance of the labyrinth by religious communities and congregations, especially in America, is the perceived heritage of the labyrinth form and the supposed practices associated with it. The fact that these labyrinth symbols were in widespread use in the medieval church eight hundred years ago not only provides validity for the form, but allows the modern pilgrim to participate in an "authentic" medieval Christian ritual. This is not some new-fangled, new-age invention, but a revival of an established and respected practice. Many people have walked this same pattern of pathways in their lifetime and the labyrinth provides a direct connection to those people and a continuity that transcends time, language, and differing liturgical traditions. A key reason for its acceptance is that because of its broad appeal, the labyrinth invites people of all ages to share a common experience. The importance of its role in building communities should not be underestimated, as bridging the interests of diverse congregations is one of the biggest challenges facing churches today.

For those seeking a less overtly, or even non-Christian, experience, the classical labyrinth form is admirably suited and likewise comes with a time-tested background from which to draw for inspiration. The worldwide distribution of this form and the wealth of folklore and traditions that accompanies it, wherever it occurs, has become instrumental in presenting and adapting the labyrinth to each new location and circumstance that it encounters. This multi-cultural approach is especially attractive and popular, and provides numerous opportunities to reach out and provide bridges between seemingly disparate sections of the community.

But what do people experience when they walk the labyrinth? Many report that their lives have changed for the better, saying that walking the labyrinth has brought them increased calm, clarifying insight, and spiritual rejuvenation. For many, the labyrinth is a pathway of prayer, an opportunity to connect with the Divine while traversing a human course, and, as such, gives opportunity to contemplate the magic and mystery of one's existence. Despite its lofty claims, the labyrinth continues to invite soulful expression, release,

BELOW *Appealing to a broad cross section of the community, the labyrinths installed at retreat centres across America have become popular gathering place for people of all faiths and persuasions.*

and healing, not with weighty dogma, but with the charms of delight and curiosity. Perhaps it is this interaction with what cannot be understood and explained, that so appeals to our impoverished postmodern imaginations.

Using the labyrinth as a tool for a walking meditation and prayer allows individuals to share a common space while going through an individuated experience. It breaks the isolation that so commonly accompanies the working through of intense emotions such as grief or catharsis. Labyrinth walking in retreat settings and pilgrimages offers the individual walker spiritual companionship and provides a visible metaphor for community and connection. Sharing the labyrinth path with other walkers gives a tangible illustration that one is not alone, either on the spiralling path or in life.

The lure of the labyrinth, as well as the magic of the maze, has ensnared humankind for thousands of years. As we progress into this new millennium, that fascination has certainly not abated – indeed it shows every sign of continuation.

GAZETTEER OF MAZES AND LABYRINTHS

The following list of mazes and labyrinths from around the world are but a small selection of the examples that are open to the public. Consult the websites given on page 172 for further information on mazes in your part of the world, and for seasonal maize mazes, etc.

USA AND CANADA

A*mazing Chicago Navy Pier, Chicago, Illinois. State-of-the-art mirror maze that has been based on the architecture of the city.

Bells Corners United Church Nepean, Ontario. Church and community project paving labyrinth. Open at all times and wheelchair accessible.

Dole Plantation Maze Kamehameha Highway, Wahiawa, Hawaii. Huge hedge maze, based on the theme of pineapples!

Governor's House Williamsburg, Virginia. Hedge maze, planted in 1935, in the historic town of Williamsburg. (Undergoing replanting at the time of writing.)

Grace Cathedral San Francisco, California. Two replicas of the Chartres Cathedral labyrinth, one in the cathedral, one outside.

International Folk Art Museum Santa Fe, New Mexico. Pavement labyrinth situated in museum courtyard with stunning mountain backdrop.

BELOW *A hedge maze in the gardens at Schoteshof, Belgium.*

New Harmony Indiana. Historic hedge maze and modern replica of the Chartres Cathedral labyrinth in park setting.

Norton Museum of Art West Palm Beach, Florida. "Theseus and Minotaur" pavement maze and large turf labyrinth.

Riverwalk Park Naperville, Illinois. Beautiful pavement replica of the Chartres Cathedral labyrinth in riverside park location.

Sibley Park Oakland, California. A collection of modern stone labyrinths built in dramatic locations by local enthusiasts.

Sparrow Healing Garden Lansing, Michigan. Elegant Chartres Cathedral labyrinth replica, open to the public at Sparrow Hospital.

Trinity Church Wall Street, Manhattan, New York. Painted labyrinth on the South Plaza of Wall Street; popular with office workers.

UK

AMazeing Hedge Maze Symonds Yat West, Herefordshire. Charming hedge maze with museum of mazes and puzzle shop.

Archbishop's Maze Greys Court, Henley, Oxfordshire. Spiritually inspired brick-and-stone path labyrinth set in turf.

Bath Festival Maze Beazer Gardens, Bath, Somerset. Elliptical stone pathway maze in a delightful riverside location.

Chinese Puzzle Maze Blackpool Pleasure Beach, Lancashire. Dramatic maze with water features set among roller coasters.

Dower House Garden Morville Hall, Shropshire. Turf labyrinth situated amid beautiful historically themed gardens.

Earth and Wild Flower Labyrinth Tapton Park, Chesterfield, Derbyshire. Huge land art labyrinth installation on a hillside.

Glendurgan House Falmouth, Cornwall. Historic hedge maze with unusual sweeping design, set in beautiful gardens.

Hazlehead Park Aberdeen, Scotland. Large traditional hedge maze, planted in 1935.

Hampton Court Palace East Molesey, Surrey. Probably the oldest surviving hedge maze in the world, planted in 1690.

Hever Castle Edenbridge, Kent. Hedge maze and new water maze set in the beautiful grounds of an historic castle.

Leeds Castle Maidstone, Kent. Splendid hedge maze with innovative underground grotto running beneath.

Les Jardins de la Mer St. Helier, Jersey. Remarkable water maze with over 200 water fountains forming its walls.

Longleat House Wiltshire. Three hedge mazes, the "Labyrinth of Love," and a splendid mirror maze. An essential pilgrimage.

Peacemaze Castlewellan Forest Park, County Down, N. Ireland. Huge yew maze, symbolizing the peace process in Ireland.

Saffron Walden Essex. A 17th-century turf labyrinth on the town common and a restored hedge maze in Bridge End Gardens.

NETHERLANDS

De Doolhof Ruurlo. Classic hedge maze planted in 1890. A copy of Hampton Court, with wide paths.

Drielandenpunt Vaals. Dramatic large hedge maze with water features at the point where three countries meet.

Dúndelle Bakkeveen. Wooden, metal, and stone mazes in an entertainment park dedicated to mazes.

St. Servaaskerk Maastricht. Two beautiful 19th-century pavement labyrinths in St. Servaas Church.

FRANCE

Amiens Cathedral Picardy. Late19th-century restoration of the original 13th-century octagonal pavement labyrinth.

Château de Cormatin Cormatin, Burgundy. Beautifully restored hedge maze surrounded by water.

Chartres Cathedral Eure-et-Loir. The best-preserved medieval pavement labyrinth, although often covered by chairs.

Jardin des Plantes Paris. Hedge maze with central summerhouse. Planted in the 18th century, restored in 1990.

Labyrinthus Reignac-sur-Indre, near Tours, Indre-et-Loire. Huge maize maze planted annually since 1997 on the same site.

St. Quentin Basilica Picardy. A 15th century copy of the labyrinth at Amiens. Well preserved and usually uncovered.

ITALY

San Vitale Basilica Ravenna. Small pavement labyrinth inlaid in coloured marble.

Villa Barbarigo Vansanzibio, near Venice. Late-17th-century hedge maze surviving in good condition.

Villa Pisani Stra, near Padua. Historic hedge maze with central tower and spiral staircases; built in 1720.

GERMANY

Altjessnitz near Bitterfeld, Sachsen-Anhalt. The oldest hedge maze in German – still popular and well tended.

Das Rad Eilenriede Forest, Hannover. Beautiful historic turf labyrinth in a forest clearing with a mature tree at the centre.

Herrenhausen Gardens Hannover. Fine restored late-17th-century gardens with an octagonal hedge maze added in 1937.

AUSTRIA
Schönbrunn Palace Gardens Vienna. Recently replanted section of a huge historic hedge maze.

SWITZERLAND
Labyrinthplatz Zeughaushof im Kasernenareal, Zurich. A labyrinth formed of flower beds and shrubs in a public square on the site of a former military academy.

SPAIN
Laberint d'Horta Park Barcelona. Beautifully restored hedge maze with fountains and statuary in a delightful setting.

PORTUGAL
Conimbríga Four Roman mosaic labyrinths preserved within the Roman ruins around the town.

SCANDINAVIA
Egeskov Fyn, Denmark. Fine historic hedge maze and huge modern bamboo hedge maze with central observation tower.

Labyrinthia Rodelund, Jutland, Denmark. Wooden panel maze and stone labyrinth with displays and puzzle shop. Website: www.labyrinthia.dk

Lejre Research Centre Sjælland, Denmark. Stone labyrinth, built 1979, overlooking a reconstructed Iron Age village.

Trällebergs Slott Ulmekärr, Bohuslän, Sweden. Beautifully preserved stone labyrinth in an area rich with prehistoric remains.

Trojaborg Visby, Gotland, Sweden. Historic stone labyrinth, just north of the walled town of Visby.

AUSTRALIA
Hedgend Maze Albert Road, Healesville, Victoria. Giant hedge maze, rainbow maze, mini-golf, tearooms, and more.

Kryal Castle Maze Warrenheip, Ballarat, Victoria. Circular brick wall maze with battlements and viewing platforms. Regular events.

Tazmazia Staverton Road, Promised Land, Tasmania. Four hedge and two brick-path mazes; the largest collection in Australia.

NEW ZEALAND
Te Ngae Park Rotorua, North Island. Wooden panel maze. Also, a large hedge maze on nearby Te Ngae Road.

The Great Maze South Highway, Wanaka, South Island. The original wooden panel maze, built 1973 and still going strong.

RESOURCES

The phenomenal success of the Internet has seen many hundreds of maze and labyrinth related websites appearing in recent years. The following list of recommended sites will hopefully provide a range of information, as well as links to many other sites.

INFORMATION-BASED
Labyrinthos www.labyrinthos.net - International maze and labyrinth resource centre, photo library and archive. Maze & labyrinth design, consultancy and tours. Publisher of *Caerdroia*.

Labyrinths in Austria www.das-labyrinthe.at & www.labyrinthe.at

Labyrinths in Germany www.begehbare-labyrinthe.de & www.mymaze.de

Labyrinths in the Netherlands www.doolhoven.nl

Labyrinths in Switzerland www.labyrinth-project.ch

The Labyrinth Society www.labyrinthsociety.org – The international society for enthusiasts, conferences, and events, etc.

Worldwide Labyrinth Locator www.veriditas.labyrinthsociety.org - Online database of labyrinths worldwide.

LABYRINTH SERVICES
Labyrinth Enterprises www.labyrinthenterprises.com - Portable and permanent labyrinths.

Paths of Peace www.pathsofpeace.com – Portable labyrinths and consultancy.

Paxworks www.paxworks.com - Portable labyrinths and more.

Relax For Life www.relax4life.com - Finger labyrinths.

Santa Rosa Labyrinth Foundation www.srlabyrinthfoundation.com – Labyrinth consultancy.

TLS Labyrinth Market www.tlslabyrinthmarket.co.uk – Labyrinth related products and services.

Veriditas www.veriditas.net - Labyrinth facilitator training and pilgrimages.

MAZE AND LABYRINTH BUILDERS
Adrian Fisher www.mazemaker.com – Maze design, development, and management; mirror, colour, and maize mazes.

Alex Champion www.earthsymbols.com – Land art and labyrinth design and construction.

Jim Buchanan www.landartist.co.uk – Land art and labyrinths.

Marty Kermeen www.labyrinthsinstone.com - Custom built labyrinths in pavement and stone.

BIBLIOGRAPHY

The following titles are for the most part still in print or readily available through libraries. They provide a selection of reading to suit all tastes and interests.

Artress, Lauren. *Walking a Sacred Path – Rediscovering the Labyrinth as a Spiritual Tool*, New York, Riverhead Books, 1995.
A classic introduction to the labyrinth and its role in the field of spiritual psychology.

Attali, Jacques. *The Labyrinth in Culture and Society*, Berkeley, California, North Atlantic Books, 1999.
Historically muddled, but thought-provoking, study of the philosophy and function of mazes and labyrinths.

Caerdroia – the Journal of Mazes & Labyrinths. First published in 1980, this international journal provides a forum for scholars and enthusiasts alike. Details available from Labyrinthos, 53 Thundersley Grove, Thundersley, Essex SS7 3EB, UK.

Candolini, Gernot. *Das Geheimnisvolle Labyrinth*, Augsburg, Germany, Pattloch, 1999.
Well-illustrated German-language study of labyrinths.

Curry, Helen. *The Way of the Labyrinth: A Powerful Meditation for Everyday Life*, New York, Penguin Compass, 2000.
A guide to using the labyrinth in personal spiritual practice, as well as in ceremony and ritual for larger groups and communities.

Fisher, Adrian and Gerster, Georg. *The Art of the Maze*, London, Weidenfeld & Nicolson, 1990.
Fully illustrated guide to mazes and labyrinths worldwide. Good detail of the early works of Adrian Fisher and Randoll Coate's.

Fisher, Adrian and Loxton, Howard. *Secrets of the Maze,* London, Thames & Hudson, 1997.
Large format book of mazes from around the world, with puzzles and solutions.

Geoffrion, Jill Kimberly Hartwell. *Praying the Labyrinth & Living the Labyrinth* Cleveland, Ohio, Pilgrim Press, 1999/2000.
Questions to guide a pilgrim's journey on the labyrinth are offered along with scriptural selections to broaden the context.

Kern, Hermann. *Through the Labyrinth*, (ed. Ferré, Robert and Saward, Jeff), Munich, Prestel, 2000.
Definitive scholarly catalogue of historic labyrinths from around the world, now translated to English and updated.

Jaskolski, Helmut. *The Labyrinth: Symbol of Fear, Rebirth, and Liberation*, Boston, Massachusetts and London, Shambhala, 1997.
Reflective and playful study of the labyrinth motif ranging from ancient myths and medieval tales to modern fiction.

Lonegren, Sig. *Labyrinths: Ancient Myths & Modern Uses*, New York, Sterling Publishing, 2001.
Instructional labyrinth workbook with wide-ranging study of labyrinth mythology, earth energies, and suggestions for practical usage.

Matthews, W. H. *Mazes and Labyrinths – Their History & Development*, New York, Dover Publications, 1970.
The classic study of the subject, and still full of facts and surprising snippets of information.

Pennick, Nigel. *Mazes and Labyrinths*, London, Robert Hale, 1990.
A wide-ranging study of maze and labyrinth history, especially in Europe.

Reed Doob, Penelope. *The Idea of the Labyrinth from Classical Antiquity through the Middle Ages,* Ithaca, NY, Cornell University Press, 1990.
Scholarly study of labyrinths from Classical antiquity through the medieval period, especially in texts and literature.

Saint-Hilaire, Paul de. *L'universe Secret du Labyrinthe,* Paris, Robert Laffont, 1992.
French-language guide to mazes and labyrinths, especially in Europe. Historically unreliable, but with extensive gazetteer.

Sands, Helen Raphael. *Labyrinth: Pathway to Meditation and Healing*, London, Gaia, 2000.
Aesthetically beautiful discussion of labyrinth design, history, and use. Includes clear instructions for creating labyrinths and open-ended suggestions for possible construction materials.

Saward, Jeff. *The Atlas of Labyrinths*, London, Gaia, 2002.
Lavishly illustrated guide to the history of mazes and labyrinths from around the world.

Simpson, Liz. *Finding Fulfilment*, London, Piatkus, 2000.
A broad outline for a self-guided process using the labyrinth to promote healthy change in one's life.

Westbury, Virginia. *Labyrinths – Ancient Paths of Wisdom and Peace*, Sydney, Australia, Lansdowne Publishing, 2001.
A nicely illustrated introduction to the labyrinth revival, with insight into the characters and reasons behind it all.

Wright, Craig. *The Maze and the Warrior,* Cambridge, Massachusetts, Harvard University Press, 2001.
Scholarly study of the labyrinth symbol in medieval and renaissance architecture, theology, and music.

INDEX

Page numbers in *italics* indicate an
illustration or caption only

ACKNOWLEDGMENTS

Mitchell Beazley would like to acknowledge and thank all those who have kindly supplied photographs for inclusion in this book.

Acknowledgements in Page Order
Key: a above, b below, l left, r right

1 Frank Spooner Pictures Ltd/Frederic Reglain/Gamma, 2 E & E Picture Library/Dorothy Burrows, 4 Georg Gerster/Network, 6–7 Jeff Saward/Labyrinthos, 8–9 Stone/Jason Hawkes, 10 Charles Walker Collection, 12–13 Georg Gerster/Network, 14–15, 16 l & r, 17 Jeff Saward/Labyrinthos, 18 Bayerische Staatsbibliothek Munich, 19 AKG London/Erich Lessing, 20–21, 21r, 22–3, 23a, 24–5 Jeff Saward/Labyrinthos, 26 Bridgeman Art Library/Fitzwilliam Museum, University of Cambridge, UK, 27 Dumbarton Oaks, Studies in Landscape Architecture, Photo Archive, 28 Bridgeman Art Library/Isabella Stewart Gardner Museum, Boston, Massachusetts, USA, 28–9 Fortean Picture Library, 30–31 Jeff Saward/Labyrinthos, 32 Clive Nichols Garden Pictures, 33 Bridgeman Art Library/Musee Condé, Chantilly, France, 34 Georg Gerster/Network, 35 Fortean Picture Library, 36, 37 Jeff Saward/Labyrinthos, 38–9 Stone/John Chard, 40a & b Fons Schaefers, 41 Georg Gerster/Network, 42–3a Garden Picture Library/Nick Meers, 43 Harpur Garden Library/Jerry Harpur, 44 Frank Spooner Pictures/Gamma/Aldo Pavan, 45 Bridgeman Art Library, 46–7 National Trust Photographic Library/Stephen Robson, 48–9a, 49b, 50 Georg Gerster/Network, 51 Robert Harding Picture Library/David Beatty, 52, 53 Adrian Fisher Maze Design, 54 Andrew Lawson Photography, 55 Gernot Candolini, 56 Georg Gerster/Network, 56–7 Georg Gerster/Network, 58–9a Frank Spooner Pictures Ltd/Frederic Reglain/Gamma, 59b E & E Picture Library, 60 Great Adventures Corn Mazes, 61 Adrian Fisher Maze Design, 62 Georg Gerster/Network, 63 The Ronald Grant Archive, 64–5 Wookey Hole Caves Ltd, 66–7 Hever Castle Ltd, 67r Adrian Fisher Maze Design, 68–9 Georg Gerster/Network, 70 Ole Jensen/Labyrinthia, 71, 72–3 Adrian Fisher Maze Design,

73 Georg Gerster/Network, 74–5 Jeff Saward/Labyrinthos, 76, 77 Adrian Fisher Maze Design, 78–9, 81, 82–3 Georg Gerster/Network, 84–5b John Comino-James, 85a Artistic Pavers Inc/Marty Kermeen, 86–7 Swarovski Kristallwelten/Kurt Mayer, 88 Labyrinthos/Jeff Saward, 89 Artistic Pavers Inc/Marty Kermeen, 90–91, 92 Georg Gerster/Network, 93 Gernot Candolini, 94, 95 Adrian Fisher Maze Design, 96–7 Georg Gerster/Network, 98–9 Garden Exposures Photo Library/Andrea Jones, 100–101 John Glover, 101 Andrew Lawson Photography, designer Celia Haddon, 102 Gernot Candolini, 103a & b John Glover, 104 Harpur Garden Library/Marcus Harpur, 105 Cindy A Pavlinac/Sacred Land Photography, 106, 107 Gernot Candolini, 108a & b John Glover, 110 Gernot Candolini, 110–11 Andrew Lawson Photography, designer Ivan Hicks, 112a Cindy A Pavlinac/Sacred Land Photography, 112–13b Andrew Lawson Photography, 114 Cindy A Pavlinac/Sacred Land Photography, 115 St. Louis Labyrinth Project/Robert Ferré, 116 Ole Jensen/Labyrinthia, 117 Cindy A Pavlinac/Sacred Land Photography, 118 Eye Ubiquitous/Paul Seheult, 119a Cindy A. Pavlinac/Sacred Land Photography, 119b, 120–21 Jeff Saward/Labyrinthos, 122–3 Artistic Pavers Inc/Marty Kermeen, 124a Georg Gerster/Network, 124–5, 126–7 Jeff Saward/Labyrinthos, 128–9 Fortean Picture Library, 130, 131 Peter Strauss, 132–3 John Glover, 133a, 134, 135, 136–7 Cindy A Pavlinac/Sacred Land Photography, 138 Jeff Saward/Labyrinthos, 139 Chris Parsons, 140, 141 Marianne Ewaldt, 142–3 Jeff Saward/Labyrinthos, 144–5, 146–7 Garden Exposures Photo Library/Andrea Jones, 148–9 Jeff Saward/Labyrinthos, 150–51 St. Louis Labyrinth Project/Robert Ferré, 152, 153, 154–5, 156 Cindy A Pavlinac/Sacred Land Photography, 157 Gernot Candolini, 158l Cindy A. Pavlinac/Sacred Land Photography, 158r, 159, 160, 161, 162–3 Jeff Saward/Labyrinthos, 164–5 Adrian Fisher Maze Design, 166 Jeff Saward/Labyrinthos, 168 Cindy A Pavlinac/Sacred Land Photography, 169 Gernot Candolini, 170 Garden Exposures Photo Library/Andrea Jones.